The Amazing Basketball
Career of
KARL
MALONE

SPECIAL DELIVERY

by Clay Latimer

ADDAX
PUBLISHING
GROUP
Lenexa, KS

3/2022

Published by Addax Publishing Group Inc.
Copyright © 1999 by Clay Latimer
Edited by Greg Echlin and Nelson Elliott
Designed by Randy Breeden
Cover Design by Jerry Hirt

For Information address:
Addax Publishing Group
8643 Hauser Drive, Suite 235, Lenexa, KS 66215

ISBN: 1-886110-64-6

Distributed to the trade by Andrews McMeel Publishing
4520 Main Street
Kansas City, MO 64111

1 3 5 7 9 10 8 6 4 2

Printed in the USA

Library of Congress Cataloging-in-Publication Data

Latimer, Clay, 1952-
    Special delivery : the amazing career of Karl Malone / by Clay
Latimer.
        p.   cm.
    ISBN 1-886110-64-6
    1. Malone, Karl. 2. Basketball players—United States—Biography.
    3. Utah Jazz (Basketball team)   I. Title.
    GV884.M18L38 1999
    796.323'092—dc21
    [B]   98-43524
                                                                       CIP

Dedication:

To Loraine

Malone had a lot to learn in his rookie season, but he was an intimidating presence, nonetheless, even for Michael Cooper and his Los Angeles Lakers "Showtime" attack. *Photo by Steve Dykes (AP).*

Table of Contents

The Amazing Basketball Career of KARL MALONE

SPECIAL DELIVERY

by Clay Latimer

Acknowledgments

Most books are collaborative efforts, and this one is no exception.

The list of thanks should start with the *Salt Lake Tribune* and *Deseret News* and the work - over the years - of Steve Luhm, Brad Rock, Dick Rosetta, Lex Hemphill, Kurt Kragthorpe, Lee Benson, Loren Jorgensen, Richard Evans, Gordon Monson, Linda Fantin, Scott Pierce and Doug Robinson. I trust I've kept their reporting and commentary in perspective.

I'd also be remiss not to credit *Sports Illustrated, Sport, Sporting News, Inside Sports, Playboy, USA Today, Lindy's Basketball, Slam* and other publications too numerous to mention.

Thanks also to several illuminating books including *Stockton to Malone! The Rise of the Utah Jazz* by Roland Lazenby, *The Golden Boys* by Cameron Stauth, *Loose Balls* by Terry Pluto, *Tall Tales* by Terry Pluto, *The Jordan Rules* by Sam Smith, *Michael Jordan* by Mitchell Krugel, *Bad as I Wanna Be* by Dennis Rodman, *Hang Time* by Bob Greene, *Wilt* by Wilt Chamberlain, *Jordan* by Mitchell Krugel, *Outrageous!* by Charles Barkley, *The Breaks of the Game* by David Halberstam, *My Life* by Magic Johnson, *Drive* by Larry Bird.

I'm also indebted to the people at Addax Publishing.

Introduction

When Karl Malone arrived in Salt Lake City in 1985, he couldn't make a free throw, hit a jumper, decipher a game plan, and he lacked the emotional resources and ruthlessness to make himself over into a first-rank power forward, according to his plentiful critics.

The Utah Jazz, meanwhile, was a burlesque of an NBA franchise.

How then, did Malone and the Jazz take over much of the hoop world? The answers comprise one of the most fascinating sports stories in recent decades.

The cast of characters is as colorful as it is varied: a wise country mom (Shirley Turner); a wise-crackin' rotund coach (Frank Layden); a wild-eyed owner (Larry Miller); a remarkably unique city (Salt Lake City); a tough edgy coach (Jerry Sloan) - as well as a wily point guard (John Stockton), who teamed with Malone to write a novel new chapter for the NBA record book.

But the ultimate character is Karl Malone, who is a truck driver, farmer, Big Time wrestler, doting father, Generation X enemy, and Mr. Olympian body builder - as well as the greatest power forward ever.

I started covering the NBA just as Malone's apprenticeship was ending, and his best days beginning. That was more than a decade ago, and the Mailman's still delivering, no matter the zip code.

Chapter One

The Greatest Power Forward Ever

What could be as humbling to a proud, macho superstar like Karl Malone than to be dunked on with mocking ease during a mere summer pick-up game?

Not much.

In fact, a worse scene was unimaginable to Malone, especially when the pick-up game was actually an intra squad Dream Team scrimmage in Europe, and Charles Barkley was the dunker.

"You gonna let him get away with it?" Michael Jordan asked him.

Foolish question.

The big machinery had already been set in motion. On the next possession Malone caught a pass from Jordan, and without a particle of reticence, humbled the man who'd humbled him with a fly-over jam of his own. Since the mid 1980s, Malone and Barkley have been playing a one-on-one game for a piece of history, combining grace and speed with hard-boiled machismo.

They're too big for smaller defenders, too fast for bigger defenders and they're willing to mortgage their bodies for a molar-loosening dunk. They're willing to do that to block a dunk.

In fact, Malone and Barkley have revolutionized the power forward position, which was once the domain of finesse-less head-bangers with single-digit scoring averages.

In the process, they've also become the best power forwards ever - and maybe the shape of things to come too.

"I started playing basketball seriously in the early 80s; I wasn't what would you call a student of the game," Malone said. "I never even heard the term power forward until I got here with the Jazz. In college ...I saw power forwards weren't scoring 25 points a game. So I figured we weren't supposed to.

"I came along at a time, and I'm sure Charles will say the same thing, when they were starting to experiment with power forwards, so to speak. And I just happened to be a guy who was playing the power forward position. There were great forwards who played the game before I did, but they didn't run the plays like they've run them for me and Charles since we came into the league."

Traditionally, guards concentrated on passing and shooting and other finesse-related skills, as did small forwards like Alex English, who actually wrote a couple books of poetry. Centers were, well, centers.

Power forwards did the dirty work: setting picks, hauling down rebounds, giving and receiving beatings, giving off bad vibes. A more indelicate job description might be "hatchet man."

Spencer Haywood and Elvin Hayes tempered the sullen image by becoming gunners as well as bangers in the mid and late 70s. But the scoring power forward became as obsolete as red-white-and-blue basketballs in the early 80s.

Then came the flying buttresses.

"Malone was the prototype forward," Jazz guard John Stockton said. "Like they were saying about Lawrence Taylor at linebacker, he was the shape of things to come. His ability to score inside and outside is pretty well noted but there's also his ability to run the floor on the fast break.

"I've watched a hundred times when he gets a rebound, outlets it to me and then beats me down to the other end of the court to get an open lay-up. Over the course of the game, he'll wear you down."

Added Barkley: "Can't nobody on the planet guard me."

At first, Malone and Barkley were typical power forwards in the stolid tradition of Bob Pettit, Dave DeBusschere and Maurice Lucas.

Malone was known as the Rimwrecker at Louisiana Tech, which seemed an apt name to the team's managers, who had to clean up the fiberglass shards after he'd shattered another backboard.

At Auburn, Barkley was known for his equatorial waist line and Herculean strength.

"Once he dunked the ball so hard that he moved the entire basket support, which was held in place by two 300-pound cement blocks," Auburn coach Sonny Smith said in Barkley's book, *Outrageous!*

"I'm cussin' and tellin' everybody to come over and help get the blocks back in place, when Charles pushed me out of the way, walked to the goal, and moved the blocks himself! He then straightened the goal and put both of those 300-pound blocks back in place."

In his first NBA season, Malone shot just 48.1% from the free-throw line, couldn't hit the Great Salt Lake with a jumper, and provided only occasional flashes of his advancing brilliance.

In his first season, Barkley averaged 14 points and 8.5 rebounds a game and played a significant role in the Philadelphia 76ers playoff run. But he was only marginally the player he would become.

But they were both in take-off phase.

Jazz coach Frank Layden, who saw Malone's raw potential, made the Mailman his go-to scorer, a role that would become the cornerstone of his game. Meanwhile, Malone built a weight room in his home and his body into a mass of muscle.

"Only the strong survive," he said. "If you're weak in the jungle, somebody's going to eat you. When you're weak on the basketball court, everybody knows that and everybody takes their shots."

During his third season, Malone averaged 25.9 points per game in the first half of the season and 29.4 in the second; 37.7 minutes per game in the first half and 40. 3 in the second; and his rebounds increased from 10.9 to 13.2.

In his third season, Barkley averaged 20 points and 12.5 rebounds per game and dazzled the league with his odd combination of talents.

By the late 80s, a new order had overtaken the hoop world.

"Barkley and Malone have a lot to do with how the game is played today," Chris Webber said.

One moment Barkley was head-butting Rick Mahorn to psyche up for a game; the next he was spinning past a 7-footer for a dunk; the one after that he was leading the break like a point guard.

"To be that big and powerful and that quick up and down the floor, he's definitely an enigma," Mychal Thompson said.

One moment Malone was Greco-wrestling with a teammate in the playful Jazz locker room, the next he was backing a 7-footer into the paint with muscular dexterity, the one after that he was racing up court with uncommon grace.

"Karl is the prototype for everything - mental toughness, shooting, rebounding, work ethic," added Atlanta Hawks general manager Pete Babcock said.

Malone and Barkley had changed the game, but where was the game going?

"I think in the 60s and 70s teams were looking for 'basketball players' - basketball skills only," Pat Riley told *Sports Illustrated* in 1987. "You had to know how to play basketball; they aren't as interested in athletic ability as we are today. The whole thing has changed in the past 10 or 12 years, to the point where coaches are looking for physical specimens. I don't say that coldly. We're looking for great athletes. A big guy - he's strong, he's filled out, he runs, he jumps. Then we teach him how to play the game.

"You've got guys who are fearless, guys who are 6-8, 230 and get the ball on the wing and say, 'Hey, I'm taking it to the rim and I'm not avoiding anybody.' Hell, 15 years ago that guy would go in for a layup in that situation and someone might step in and take a charge. Now you've got guys who are going to block dunks."

Others believed Malone and Barkley were aberrations. Sure, they can shoot from the perimeter, throw no-look passes, put the ball on the floor during the break, score on an artful finger roll, sink a hook and shoot the fadeaway jumper.

But how many men with their size will ever do that again? "It's no secret that the game is changing, that guys are getting bigger, stronger and faster," former Jazz center Danny Schayes said. "There is great athleticism. But I don't know if it's the trend of the future, because how many Charles Barkleys and Karl Malones are out there? I mean, it's not that you can find 300 guys that big and that fast."

Meanwhile Malone and Barkley continued their one-on-one war, though they rarely faced each other in games.

"Any time against Karl it gets somewhat personal," Barkley told *Sport*. "Even though we're friends, I think both of us want to be considered the best power forward."

In 1992, in preparation for the Olympics, *Sports Illustrated* asked coaches and general managers, "If you were starting a team and could take either (Barkley or Malone), whom would you prefer?"

Malone won 15-7, primarily because of Barkley's

penchant for controversy.

"Charles is better when he wants (to play hard), but you never know when that's going to be. I'll take Karl," an Eastern Conference executive said.

"If it was just basketball you were talking about, I'd go with Barkley," a Western Conference exec said.

Only one respondent believed Malone was a better player.

But as the 90s progressed, so did Malone, who approached every season with the compulsion of a chronic overture.

In the 1993 all-star game, he scored 28 points, pulled down 10 rebounds and was named MVP. In 1997, at age 33, he became the oldest man ever to win the NBA's MVP award.

The following season he averaged 27 points per game, shot .530 from the floor, .761 from the line, averaged 10.3 rebounds per game, dealt out 3.9 assists a game, had 96 steals and blocked 70 shots.

In the 1997 and 1998 Championship Finals against the Chicago Bulls, even Malone's harshest critics gave him his due.

Why not? Malone was the offensive and defensive force on a team that had reached three Western Conference finals and two NBA finals in the 90s.

"All your life you dream of being a sports figure - sort of like a Superman or a Spiderman," he said in *American Health* magazine. "Then all of a sudden you're one of them. To compete against another player, that makes it all worthwhile.

"It motivates me to play hard, to do the things I need

to do. I think basketball players are the best athletes in the world. The running, the cutting, the rebounding, the jumping: it's non-stop. Going out there and competing over an 82-game schedule, that makes me proud. I love representing my team, night in, night out, because I've made my work into my play.

"The game of basketball is simple, really. Everybody is always trying to make up millions of plays just to make it hard. But it's not. Pass the ball to the open man and let him score. It's not hard, it's just mental. It's the guy who has, I guess, the most mental toughness - he's the guy who has the edge. You know your talent, you know what you've got. Use it to your advantage."

Maybe Barkley had seen it coming. Years before, after an off-season scrimmage, he told Malone's mother, "If I'm picking a team, Karl's my first pick."

"I snuck up on people," Malone said. "The only people who believed in me were Utah and my family. Sometimes I feel like I'm in a dream. I wake up and none of this seems possible. It all happened so fast - boom, boom, boom.

"But don't ever tell me I'll forget my roots; I'll always know where I'm from. I'm proud to be a country boy. I try to pattern my life after my mom. Since she knows life in the NBA is short, she just says, 'Have fun while it lasts.' "

Chapter Two

Country Boy

Karl Malone has scored more than 25,000 points and pulled down more than 10,000 rebounds during his NBA career, a milestone previously reached only by Wilt Chamberlain, Kareem Abdul-Jabbar, Elvin Hayes and Moses Malone.

A daunting feat?

Not to the Mailman's mother.

Shirley Turner picked 174 pounds of cotton one day, barely losing a contest to two other women, then gave birth to a son that night.

Talk about a special delivery.

Few NBA players can equal Malone's determination, resiliency and stoicism, and fewer still his mother's.

In 1989, *USA Today* picked an All-Mom Team that included Virginia Dantley (Adrian Dantley), Charcey Mae Glenn (Charles Barkley), Deloris Jordan (Michael Jordan), Mary Thomas (Isiah Thomas) and Shirley Turner.

Karl's mother should've been MVP.

The Mailman's route to the top begins with Shirley

Turner in Summerfield, La., goes through Ruston, La., proceeds to Salt Lake City, branches all over the U.S., bridges the Atlantic and Pacific oceans, and then winds back to Shirley's front porch off U.S. 167.

"My mom is my life," he said.

It was a country life, and Karl was a wild country boy.

Not to mention a mama's boy.

"He's nothing but a big old crybaby," she said. "I'd just sit him down and look him in the eye. He cried without even getting a whupping."

Malone's father, J.P. Malone, committed suicide when he was three, leaving Shirley to raise nine children by herself in Summerfield, a small town scattered over five miles in the north central part of Louisiana. Population: 600.

"Counting the chickens and cows," Karl said.

Shirley refused to stand still like a bull's eye. To put food on the table, she ran a forklift in a sawmill ($50 a week), took apart chickens in a poultry plant, cooked for another family and went on fishing and hunting forays.

When a social worker told her she qualified for welfare, Shirley shrugged her shoulders, and went on with her life in Summerfield, which was no match for her grit.

"It don't take nothing to satisfy me," Turner said. "I've got a fishing rod and bait, and I'm happy as a flea on a dog's back."

Shirley couldn't afford Karl's first basketball, which cost $2.95, so she made a down payment of 75 cents and paid the difference later. Little Karl still lacked a basket and backboard, but Shirley solved that problem too, forming a circle with her arms while standing on a chair. That was one backboard the Mailman had no desire to shatter.

"I could never repay her for all she's done," he said.

"I saw my mother wear cardboard in her shoes, just so each of us could have a good pair."

In 1975, Shirley married Ed Turner, a local plumber. Together they opened Turner's Grocery and Washateria, located seven miles from Summerfield High, and 39 from Louisiana Tech.

When Karl was 12, he and his older brother put up a backboard in the backyard, where the Mailman learned a few lessons about the x's and o's of real life, not to mention rank sibling rivalry.

"My brother used to rough me up on purpose," said Malone, who started loading hay and working in chicken houses at the same time. "I would shoot the ball and he would hit me for no reason. I would cry and he would say, 'You little sissy.' I would be fighting mad all the time. I always think back to the times I never beat him, the times I let down and he'd take advantage of it."

Malone was entering his "mannish phase," as he described it, which was bad news for neighbors, who saw Karl shoot out a window with a BB gun, demolish a watermelon patch and ride wild hogs through backyards, among other things.

The acts of rascality didn't end there.

"Another time his mama was in the hospital and Karl took the Plymouth duster for a ride with his friends," Ed said. "He rolled the car over. Karl wasn't hurt, but he was scared. He called me and said, 'Don't tell Mama. I'll tell her.' "

Karl and his brothers reveled in their devilment.

"When I was growing up, I loved to live on the edge," he said. "I loved to see how far I could push a person before he either exploded or went crazy like I was a scientist. My attitude was to push you until either your hair would fall out or your eyes came out of your head.

"If we didn't get a whupping, we just couldn't sleep at night. From when I was 12 until I was 17, if we went a day-and-a-half without getting a whupping, something was wrong with us. I never did drugs or drank, but I was just mannish as hell. My mom used to tell me: 'Boy, I brought you into this world, I can take you out.' You don't believe me? Ask my mom!"

Malone gradually began to funnel his energy into sports.

During his sophomore year, he briefly flirted with baseball.

"My first time up," he said, "the guy threw at me. He said he didn't, but I think he did. I'll never forget his name - Johnny Phillips ... I might be overreacting, but I thought I felt the thread on the ball go right across my nose.

"I said to myself, 'This is not for me.' I didn't even talk to the coach. I just sort of looked at him and walked away."

But Malone was unstoppable on the basketball court, leading Summerfield to three Class C titles with the help of younger brother Terry, a clever passer who now runs the Mailman's ranch in Arkansas.

"It was exactly like John Stockton and Karl Malone," Shirley told the *Salt Lake Tribune*. "The only difference was, Terry was left-handed."

By Karl's senior year, the Summerfield Rebels wanted to challenge the state's bigger schools. "I don't know if anybody could've beaten us. We were loaded," said principal James Scriber.

Instead, the Rebels settled for total domination, mauling over matched opponents.

Malone, who averaged more than 30 points per game, was heavily recruited by Arkansas, as well as Louisiana Tech. He was tantalizingly close to big-time ball when his plans came to a humiliating halt. He had but a 1.97 grade-point-average.

"I wanted to know what kind of grades it would take before they would stop letting me play basketball," he said.

He found out soon enough. With options dwindling, Malone decided on Tech, which was only 40 miles away from Shirley.

"He was too crazy about home," Ed Turner said.

Four years later, in Salt Lake City, Malone still couldn't break his bonds with his mother.

"He was homesick," said Shirley, who sent her son weekly shipments of Louisiana collard greens, watermelons and catfish fillets.

"That first month he was there, we had a $700 phone bill. He wanted to come home. I told him, 'Sugar, that's your job now.' "

Malone's academic problems delighted his "non-admirers" in Summerfield, who were tired of his adolescent pranks and the fury and fuss that accompanied them.

"They say, 'I told you he wasn't going to do good, I

told you he was going to be a drug addict, I told you he wasn't going to have no money,' " Malone told *Playboy*. "That's what drives me. I don't want to prove those people right. I want to make them look like asses for the rest of my life.

"I had let my family down, I had let Karl Malone down. So I was at the point where I said, 'Karl, are you going to be a loser the rest of your life or are you going to do something positive with yourself? You can either go to college or sit at home and be what everybody expects you to be, which is nothing.' "

Many figured Scriber, the principal, might have done something about Karl's grades.

"I took a real hit on that from some people," he said. "I wanted him to play, more than anybody - that was the truth. One person stood by me. That was Shirley."

Instead, Malone took out a bank loan, moved to Ruston, played intramural ball, improved his grades and settled into a normal applauseless life.

"I was confused," he said. "They told me, 'Karl Malone, you're a basketball player, but you can't play for a year.' It's like you're an inventor and you can't invent for a year.

"(But it) was the best thing that ever happened to me. My last years of high school, I was starting to think I was better than other people, that I was special and things would just come to me."

Charles Barkley made no assumptions during his freshman and sophomore years at Alabama's Leeds High, where he was undersized, overlooked and over motivated.

"He practiced basketball for the whole summer," his

mother, Charcey Mae, recalled in *Outrageous!* "There was a court right down the street from our house, but he never liked to go down there during the day when all the other kids were there and people were just standing around watching. He waited until night, after everybody had gone home, and he would play by himself for hours.

"He also asked me to buy him a jump rope. When I did, I thought he was going to jump that rope to death. He wood jump and jump, jump, jump, jump. Again he did it for hours at a time. While every other kid in the neighborhood was going to the movies or out dancing, Charles was either jumping our fences, jumping rope or, doing something to improve himself physically."

Jumping fences?

"I didn't care how dangerous it was, but my fence-jumping used to drive (my) Granny crazy," Barkley said in his book. "She tried to warn me that if I made a mistake and missed, I could mess myself up for life 'as far as having children, you know,' she used to say.

"So she'd sit on the porch and watch me, like sitting there was going to make a difference if I fell. She sat there watching me for two or three hours, back and forth. I don't know how I did it, but I truly believe those fence-jumping afternoons are what gave my legs their strength."

Basketball was life's blood for Larry Bird, who took monomania to a new level in the NBA, where he was a mass riddle to defenses.

"I (got) a basketball for Christmas once and when I unwrapped it I thought it was the greatest thing I'd ever seen in my life," he wrote in *Drive*. "It was better than a football, a bicycle or anything.

"Remember those pot-bellied stoves? I got that basketball out and played in the snow. It lost air and I couldn't dribble it. I brought it in and put it next to the stove to get it heated and then I brought it back out. It would last two or three hours that way.

"One night I left the ball by the stove by accident. I got up in the morning and discovered a basketball with bumps all over it. I kept that ball for two years because I couldn't afford a new one and when I would dribble the ball it would go this way or that."

Bird broke his ankle in his sophomore year of high school. He was sidelined for nearly the entire season. Sort of.

"I found I could still shoot free throws while I was propped up on my crutches and I turned my attention to working on my passing, which I found was possible if I hobbled around on my cast," he said.

No one worked harder on his game than Bob Cousy, who revolutionized the point-guard position with his passing magic. He was cut twice by his high school team, however, which lacerated his pride, but never his resolve.

"There were so many big guys who tried out every year, and I got lost in the shuffle," said Cousy, who was 5-8 and skinny. "I got cut my first two years, but I kept playing anywhere I could find a game - the church league, the CYO, the NY Press League.

"It was at one of those games that Coach (Lou) Grummond finally noticed me. He said, 'Why don't you come out for the team?' I didn't tell him I'd already been out twice."

For Magic Johnson, basketball was a fever dream that

often yanked him from sleep and into pre-dawn practices. "I'd dribble on the street," he wrote in *My Life*. "I'd run around the parked cars and pretend they were players on the other team. All up and down Middle Street, people used to open their windows and yell at me for waking them up. But I couldn't help it. The game was just in me."

Karl Malone, on the other hand, lacked the passion of purists like Magic and Cousy. He viewed basketball from a utilitarian angle, as a practical means to a profitable end.

While others luxuriated in the game's aesthetics, Malone pounded away at it with the semi-indifference of a day laborer.

"I know this is going to sound crazy," he said in 1991, "but I'm not totally in love with basketball. Growing up, I played the game because my brothers and sisters did. I played because I was the tallest guy in class. I was supposed to play. I didn't have the money to buy an 18-wheel (truck), so I said, 'Hey, maybe this can help.' My dream was not to play in the NBA, but by playing in the NBA, I saw I could fulfill my real dreams.

"I'll give my all while I'm playing, but I look forward to the transition into my real life."

Not surprisingly, NBA scouts had serious doubts about Malone's desire and commitment as the 1985 Draft approached, though few doubted his skill.

Tech went 19-9, 26-7 and 29-3 in the Malone years, and received NCAA bids in his final two seasons. In 1984, the Bulldogs beat Fresno State in the first round before losing to Houston. In Malone's last year, Tech was nationally ranked and beat Pittsburgh and Ohio State before losing in overtime to Oklahoma in the regional semifinals.

Malone was the biggest draw on campus his first year - as an intramural player. During his first month of varsity play, he dominated opponents like they were intramural players.

He scored 19 points during Tech's upset 62-61 win over nationally ranked James Madison at the Ball State Classic.

"He's got to be one of the best freshman in the nation," James Madison Coach Lou Campanelli said. "He has good poise, isn't afraid to mix it up under the basket, and has a good shooting touch."

During an 81-77 loss to Ball State in the championship game, Malone led all scorers with 37 points and 16 rebounds, including 20 during the stretch run, and was named the tourney's MVP.

"Once we get the ball into him," Coach Andy Russo said, "it's tough to handle him. He's progressing better than we thought he would this early. I knew he was a good one, but he's already shown some things that we couldn't believe so early in his career."

At that point, a local writer said: "If a vote was taken today, Malone would probably be named as 'The Freshman of the Year' for the league and the entire state."

But by the end of his sophomore season, Malone had become more than a parochial hero. Much more.

Indiana Coach Bobby Knight invited him to the 1984 Olympic Trials, and although he was dismissed when Knight cut the roster to 20 players, Malone certainly belonged. At the time, however, he felt insulted.

"If you were ever doing something in your life that you

thought you were pretty good at, and someone stepped up who had more authority than you and told you that you weren't good enough ....Well, it sort of upset me."

Malone's life was changing in other ways. He'd grown up fearing whites, an ancient reflex in Summerfield.

At Louisiana Tech, however, he was "adopted" by a white couple, Murray and Mabel Ruth Moore, who hired him in summers to bale hay and drive a tractor on their Arkansas farm.

"I overcame my fear (when) I met my foster pop," he said. "I don't talk much about him and his wife, but next to my own initial family, they've been the most influential people in my life."

Insecurities about his size 16 feet and height also convinced him he was not a born athlete.

"You sit back and watch those TV commentators talking about this person's body and the way that person moves on the court – carrying on about 'born athletes.' " he said. "That's a flat-out bunch of b.s. Across the board. No exceptions. Sure, God gave you something. He gave you a body and brain to run that body. He left it up to you as a person with a heart to get the potential out of that body. All those sports guys who talk that way, let 'em spend a day with me working out."

At Louisiana Tech, Malone quickly destroyed doubts about his future. Indeed, he had that unique ability to reduce a backboard to so many jillion little pieces.

Some Tech PR people retrieved them, attached them to cards which listed all of Malone's feats, and mailed them to 1,000 media members.

"Special Delivery from the Mailman," they

proclaimed.

But the nickname didn't take hold until Malone's junior year, when a hailstorm prevented Tech from playing Northeast Louisiana. In a makeup game the next night, he scored 25 points and pulled down 15 rebounds. "The Mailman Delivered," the headline read the following day.

Malone's college career included some troublesome moments, too.

In his final season, he inadvertently knocked down Rice center Dave Ramer with an elbow. Ramer suffered a depressed right cheekbone, a collapsed sinus, a hairline fracture of the jaw and was done for the year.

"Borderline criminal," Rice coach Tommy Suitts said.

Malone was horrified.

"I talked to Karl on the phone the next morning and he just broke down into tears," Shirley said. "He kept saying 'I didn't mean it.' "

But Malone pushed on as the Bulldogs moved up in the polls and then through the early rounds of the NCAA Tournament. The dream season finally came to a sour end in the Sweet 16 in Dallas on a last-second shot by Oklahoma's Wayman Tisdale.

"He was a man among boys (in college)," Coach Russo said many years later. "He was so dominating. His high school coach put him on the outside, if you can believe that. That was probably good because he established an outside shot."

Added Tech trainer Sam Wilkinson: "From day one, Karl had his priorities straight. He got himself ready to play, academically and physically."

But Malone's team was a sideshow to the Lady Techsters, who won two national women's championships during the Mailman's unprecedented tenure. When Malone was compared to Rodman, it was with Debra Rodman, Dennis' sister, one of the best rebounders in Tech history, and not her unique brother.

Only after developing into an NBA star did Malone become more famous on campus than Lady Tech stars Janice Lawrence and Pat Gant.

Some even believed the Lady Techsters could've have beaten the men's Tech team starring Malone!

"That was a sensitive issue," he said. "There was always talk around about how the girls could beat us. But they never issued the challenge. Maybe because they knew we'd kill them."

Nevertheless, Malone remains true to that school. In 1995, he donated $100,000 for a new weight room for the football program.

"Karl never let fame go to his head," Shirley Turner said. "I'm so proud of that. He hasn't changed a bit. He's the same Karl he was growing up in Louisiana. He knows God enabled him to get to where he is today and he knows God can bring him down, too."

"It's going to be hard to find a woman like my mother," he said in 1988. "The first woman who's like her - whether she's black, white, Eskimo, from Tahiti or whatever - I marry the next day."

After Stockton threw the 80-foot bomb to Malone to win Game Four of the 1997 NBA Championships, after the Jazz players had done their celebrating, Malone once again brought his mother to center stage.

"I was just one of Shirley's kids," he said.

Even then, however, Malone was often consumed by thoughts of his father, the man who disappeared when he was three. Malone concealed the cause of his death, attributing it to cancer rather than suicide.

Former New Orleans Saints quarterback Archie Manning found himself in a similar predicament. Manning grew up in Delta, Mississippi, where Buddy, his father, ran a farm machinery shop. In 1969, after battling health and business problems for a couple years, the elder Manning shot and killed himself.

After finding his father, Archie kept his mother and sister at bay, called local authorities, and then cleaned things up. A few weeks later, he began his junior season at Ole Miss.

Larry Bird enjoyed a good relationship with his father, Joe Bird, who encouraged all his kids to chase their dreams. Joe worked at the local Kimball factory, where he spray-painted pianos and organs, a job he took pride in. Even so, he repeatedly switched jobs, and spent much of his increasingly idle time with friends, drinking and telling stories, which angered his wife, who eventually sought a divorce.

The elder Bird was forced to move into his parent's house as financial problems engulfed him.

After missing some custody payments to his wife, the police came to his parents' home. Joe asked for a couple hours to sort out his bills, then called his wife.

"He got off the phone, took a shotgun and killed himself. Grandma and Grandpa were in the house at the time, but they didn't know what happened at first. When you live in the country, you hear hunters and you hear different sounds all the time. But the police came in and asked for Joe and there he was.

"People have speculated as to what would have happened if Dad had lived long enough to see my basketball success at Indiana State. I do know this much: If he'd been alive then, he and Mom would have been living in Terre Haute. It would've taken a little while, but things would have gotten a lot better. I'm sure of that."

Charles Barkley's father didn't commit suicide, but he disappeared from his life when Charles was three. The pain was overwhelming.

"Charles was always so bitter when it came his daddy," Charcey Mae said in *Outrageous!* "Even during his rookie season in the NBA, he didn't want to involve his daddy in any way. He never even mentioned his father in any story that was done about him. After a while, Frank called and asked me why Charles was treating him that way, why he was pretending like his daddy didn't exist. Can you believe that?

"I wanted to tell him. I truly wanted to tell him that."

When Barkley was in tenth grade, his father called him and said he'd sent him a Christmas gift. The present would be coming home with Charles' aunt, who lived in California and was returning to Leeds for the holidays. By Christmas Eve, Barkley's aunt had been home a couple days, and Charles hadn't received a phone call.

So he walked over to his aunt's house.

"Charles went down there and found out that his father hadn't sent him anything. In fact, his aunt didn't even know Frank was supposed to send anything. When

Charles got home, he was more hurt and upset than I had ever seen him in his life. Lord forgive me, but if I could've gotten my hands on Frank that night, I think I could've killed him. Charles said he would never ask his father for anything else as long as he lived. He never did.

"To say Charles hated his father is not an exaggeration. He called his father 'scum.' "

Added Barkley: "Thoughts of my father bugged me throughout my life. When I was young, I would see other kids with their fathers and felt empty, like I was being cheated. I missed his companionship. I missed having an older friend. It burns me up when I read these days about all the teenage boys who are becoming fathers with teenage girls, then leaving the mothers alone to raise the babies by themselves.

"And those guys who have three or four babies by different women should be castrated."

Life wasn't any easier for Isiah Thomas' family. His father left when he was three, leaving his mother to raise nine children by herself in a Chicago combat zone. Once, she had to stand at the door with a shotgun to discourage gang members from recruiting Isiah.

In 1994, Jazz owner Larry Miller publicly criticized Malone's play during a bitterly disappointing playoff run. Malone, who considers Miller a father figure, was deeply hurt by the verbal assault. In a tearful news conference, he announced his father's suicide, speaking passionately about the anger, the frustration and abandonment he felt watching Shirley raise nine children.

"It was hard to tell my secret," he said. "It took me a long time, but it was kind of like hanging over my head.

My father not being around, and I was always upset that he wasn't, and that it was his own decision. I didn't accept that, and that's what drives me now. (It) motivates me as a man, as a father and as a person."

Chapter Three

Stranger in a New World

After the Utah Jazz selected him with the 13th pick of the 1985 NBA Draft, Karl Malone walked numbly to the stage, exchanged some high fives, shook hands with NBA Commissioner David Stern and sat down to be interviewed on national TV.

Then the Mailman, who felt as if his dreams had just been knocked out of him, began weeping.

"I'm not going to lie to you," Malone said later. "When they said, 'The Utah Jazz picks Karl Malone of Louisiana Tech,' I said, 'Oh no!'

"The only thing I knew about Utah was the Mormons."

Jazz fans felt like crying, too, when Malone, his brain in a spin, told coach Frank Layden, "I'm going to do the best I can to bring a great team to the town of Utah."

"Son," Layden replied, "it's a state."

At that point, Layden realized Karl Malone needed a

father figure. Not to mention a geography lesson.

Over the years, Layden has worked as an actor, public speaker, talk-show host, women's professional basketball coach, radio analyst and after dinner speaker.

But in his heart, Layden remains a teacher, a job he held in Long Island four decades ago.

"Sometimes, I think as though I'm still a high school teacher," he said in 1984, after being named the Western Conference All-Star Game coach. "You know, homeroom, lunchroom duty - the whole bit.

"It's something I could still fall back on."

In a way, Layden did just that with Malone, making him his ultimate special-credit project on and off the court, and then making him over into a superstar.

"He's my father figure," Malone said.

But before he helped the Mailman, Layden had to save the Jazz. Because the franchise was a national joke, his clever wit, which he often turned on his own girth, turned out to be Layden's saving grace.

Twirling a trademark cigar, the Brooklyn-born wize-guy offers one-liners ala Henny Youngman.

• "I only put weight on in certain places - pizzerias, ice cream parlors, bakeries."

• "A good scorer and a good point guard should go hand-in-hand, but not from the locker room to the shower."

• "I was so ugly when I was born, the doctor slapped my mother."

• On a former player: "I told him, son, what is it with you? Is it ignorance or apathy? He said, 'Coach, I don't know and I don't care.' "

• "I happen to have an absolutely beautiful body. The only problem is that it's inside me."

• "Computers are smarter than people. Not once have I ever seen one jogging."

• "When I was in high school and the coach told us to haul your butt, it took me two trips."

• "Sometimes I get the urge to jog. When I do, I lay down and it passes."

• "I was 18 until I knew that cops in New York get paid by the city, too."

"In the early years, Frank was the glue that held the Jazz together," Jazz owner Larry Miller said. "How he did it, I don't know. He sold the Jazz to the fans, the players, the owners and the NBA. He never gave up hope. He had a lot to do with molding the franchise into what it became today. Frank was so well known for his jokes, and sometimes seen as a buffoon, that people had a tendency to overlook his acumen."

Added Layden: "The fun, the laughs we had, it was a diversion. The team was funny (and) I decided to take a Casey Stengel approach."

Layden's mother died shortly after she'd given birth to him, so he was raised by two older sisters and his father, a salty ex-boxer, who said early on: "Hey, we've all got to get behind Frank because he's got a shot at becoming somebody someday."

Layden started his coaching career at a Brooklyn high school as a player-coach because of his shrewd insights.

Then it was on to Niagara, where he roomed with teammate Hubie Brown, who later coached the New York Knicks and Atlanta Hawks, among others.

Once again, Layden was asked to coach as well as play.

"In my junior and senior years," Layden said, "the coach asked me if I could coach the freshmen. I'd sort of hoped to go on to become a lawyer. But I couldn't get accepted anyplace. I guess my basic mediocrity came out."

After army duty and several years as a prep coach, Layden became the head coach at Niagara, where he refined the talents of Calvin Murphy and guided the team to one NCAA tournament and two trips to the NIT.

In 1976, Hubie Brown hired him as his assistant coach in Atlanta. Three years later, Layden joined the Utah Jazz as general manager.

At several points, owner Sam Battistone asked Layden to succeed coach Tom Nissalke, but Layden repeatedly resisted. Eventually, however, after a long series of lateral trades, Layden decided it was time to rebuild through the draft.

So he became head coach/budget cutter in 1981.

"We've just been trying to survive and most of the decisions we make are economic decisions rather than basketball decisions. For example, (the 1983) Danny Schayes trade. We didn't want to trade Danny Schayes, but we needed the money. We just had to do it," said

Layden, who also traded 1982 No. 1 pick Dominique Wilkins to Atlanta.

"People are mistaken what your primary goal is. It's to make money. This isn't a fraternity; we have to fill a building. What you have to do is put the championship second and worry about staying in operation."

Nonetheless, three years later, in 1984, Layden was voted NBA Coach – and General Manager – of the Year.

"That was the year of the underdog," he said. "The Cubs, Padres and Jazz. If World War III had broken out, Norway would've have won."

A year before, Battistone had rewarded Layden with a 10-year contract, the longest in NBA history. In the wake of the '84 season, Layden was given an honorary degree from Niagara and a silver-gray Mercedes 380 SL from Battistone.

"Time was when admitting to being the Jazz coach was like saying you were the lookout at Pearl Harbor," Layden quipped.

Added Orlando General Manager Pat Williams: "Layden is the only coach in the league where all the other coaches were happy for him and rejoiced in his success. Now that's unusual for this gang."

One of Layden's most brilliant moves was one of his first: He hired his son, 23-year-old Scott.

His qualifications?

"I'm married to his mother," Frank said.

Nepotism has never been a high crime in the NBA. Cotton Fitzsimmons, Bill Musselman, Don Nelson and

Doug Moe all hired their sons. But as Nissalke's assistants scattered, only Frank and Scott remained on the bench. Only Scott remained after Frank was tossed in a game against the Nuggets.

"We ran the four-play every time down the floor, because that was Adrian (Dantley's) play," Scott said of his survival strategy.

A short while later Frank hired Phil Johnson and Jerry Sloan as his assistants, and Scott moved to the front office, where he eventually eclipsed even his father's contributions by engineering the prescient Stockton and Malone picks.

Odd as it seems now, several teams doubted Malone's commitment to basketball entering the draft, which is why such luminaries as Keith Lee, Ed Pinckney, Benoit Benjamin, Jon Koncak, Joe Kleine and Kenny Green preceded him.

Some around the NBA doubted his skills too.

During a pre-draft retreat in the Odgen Mountains, even the Laydens had doubt after watching Malone on tape.

"We all said, 'He's not gonna be there, so we're wasting our time. We don't have to watch any more of this,' " Frank Layden said.

When Malone fell into their lap, Frank Layden asked: "Does he have AIDS or something?"

He didn't have any such thing, but the NBA is littered with the carcasses of players with vast potential - and puny careers.

For example, when he became the first high school player to skip college and graduate directly into the NBA in 1975, Darryl Dawkins seemed destined for the Hall of Fame.

Before long, the 6-foot-11, 260-pound dunk monster was stuck on Lovetron, the planet from which he claimed to hail. Dawkins called himself Chocolate Thunder, but the rest of the team called him Manchild, emphasis on child.

In 1978, 76ers coach Billy Cunningham pulled Dawkins aside after watching him mess up. Cunningham told Dawkins he needed to grow up - fast. Dawkins nodded solemnly. As Cunningham started to walk away, Dawkins stuck his foot in front of Cunningham and tripped him.

Marvin "Bad News" Barnes was an incredibly athletic power forward, and more. Much more.

Barnes never fully understood the concept of team chemistry. In fact, he blew up the lab a few times during his strange days with the ABA's Spirits of St. Louis.

Before a practice, Barnes entered the locker room with a 9-mm gun. His teammates immediately hit the floor and stayed there. They didn't get up until Barnes proved the gun didn't contain a magazine.

Before games, Barnes snacked on massive plates of nachos, hamburgers and popcorn. Then he'd have the trainer rub him in baby oil so his body would shine. " 'News' likes to look good for his people."

Barnes paid the ballboy to shine his Rolls Royce.

"People want 'News' ' car to look good."

"News" constantly made news by routinely being fined for tardiness, insubordination and missed flights. One season the Spirits fined him $5,000 for breaking all team rules.

At West Virginia, Hot Rod Hundley liked to inspire fans by shooting from behind his back, spinning the ball on his fingertips, hanging from the rim and joking with officials.

Hundley's antics caught up with him after he was drafted by the Minneapolis Lakers. After missing a team meeting following a marathon party, Hundley and teammate Bob Leonard were summoned to the office of owner Bob Short.

Hundley was called in first and fined $1,000, or one-tenth of his salary. At the time, it was the biggest fine ever leveled, relative to salary.

As Hundley left the office, Leonard was awaiting his turn, worried sick his wife would find about his infraction.

"How much?" Leonard asked anxiously.

"A big one, baby, a big bill," Hundley replied.

"A hundred dollars?" Leonard asked.

"A thousand," Hundley said.

Tears came to Leonard's eyes.

"It's a record," Hundley said.

At that point, Leonard brightened and said, "Let's go out and celebrate."

In the summer of 1985, Malone rode on a float next

to Hundley - now the Jazz play-by-play man - during a Brigham Young anniversary parade in Salt Lake City.

"Afterwards, I asked Hundley, 'What did you think of him?' " Frank Layden said.

"'I don't know if he's big enough," Hundley said.

"You gotta be crazy! I don't know if he can play, but I know he's big enough to play power forward," Layden replied.

The point is: evaluating basketball talent is a risk-intensive business.

And there were some legitimate concerns about Malone.

Basketball, surprisingly, was not an obsession at that point; it wasn't even a consuming hobby for the Mailman, who had other career goals.

"I really wanted to be a state trooper or a truck driver," Malone said. "I played terrible in rookie camp because I just wanted to get it over with. In my first year, basketball wasn't a do-or-die situation for me.

"I would be the first to admit that I didn't take anything seriously my rookie year. I was just happy to be playing."

Malone had some nagging concerns about Utah as well.

"I was nervous when I first came to Utah," he told *Sport*. "In fact, it took me a week-and-a-half to see the first black person. And he was a bag man on the street. I was so happy to see a black face that I spoke to him for two hours."

Shortly after moving into a posh mountain home, Malone looked up and saw what appeared to be a cross on his front yard. It was actually the wooden base of an overturned Christmas tree Malone himself had placed in the trash. But as the neighborhood's sole black person, "I swore the Klan had nailed a cross in my yard. So I hit the floor and turned off the lights."

A good coach always keeps the lights on.

Denver Broncos coach Mike Shanahan, for example, went way beyond the call of duty when he became John Elway's guru in 1984. Shanahan was a 31-year-old assistant with no previous NFL experience at the time. Elway a shell-shocked second-year player.

"When I first came here and started coaching John ...he'd struggled a bit in his first year," Shanahan said.

"I put him on a weight training program and even lifted with him. We developed a close relationship, and out of that grows friendship."

Shanahan and Elway played golf, drank beers, plotted strategy, analyzed opponents, traded war stories, and if none of Denver's wide receivers could be summoned to the practice field in the off-season, Shanahan would lace up his cleats and play catch with the $5 million quarterback at a nearby park.

"There's a bond there, a trust there. There's a belief in one another," Shanahan said. "I think that really helps a coach when a player knows you care about him. You've been through the wars together. He knows how you react under pressure. He knows that when the going gets tough, you're going to be there for him. You're not going to turn your back and I think those are special bonds."

Layden adopted the same approach with Malone, because he had to. During his rookie season, the Mailman made fewer than half his free throws, was a poor shooter from the field, screamed at refs and fans and produced more questions than answers for a team hungry for victories.

They talked by phone on the days the Jazz didn't practice or play and often met for breakfast and exchanged letters during the off-season. On team flights they always sat in adjacent seats. "You always sit next to the guy who can take you to the mountain-top," Layden said.

"X's and O's are the easy part of coaching. Equate coaching a young player to convincing a child to jump into a swimming pool: You have to nurture them. Once they do, they realize it's not that bad.

"Every day I tried to touch Karl - a pat on the back, a handshake, a loud scream. "

Jack Gardner, former University of Utah coach and later a Jazz consultant, said Layden was the right man at the right time.

"Remember, this isn't the richest team in the league," he told *Sports Illustrated*, ''and it doesn't have a lot of big stars. But Frank has a special savvy with the players. He'll pray over them, and he'll feed them emotional sugar when they need it. And he'll kick them in the ass when they've got it coming. That's what does it."

As a tribute to his coach, Malone wrote "Frank" on the heels of his basketball shoes, and wore jersey No. 26, Layden's high school number, in his second All-Star game appearance.

"Frank is like a father to me," he said. "The only difference from being a father is that he doesn't go home with me at night. So many coaches tell you to bust your butt all the time, then they don't have time for you as a person. You know, athletes are sensitive. We want friends, too.

"He never hollered or got in my face or applied a ball-and-chain approach to me. He just told me I had the potential to be good, maybe great. I needed to hear that. He made me aware of what I could achieve if I extended myself. He helped me get serious about the game."

Jazz star Adrian Dantley also tried to influence Malone.

"At the rookie orientation, they said, 'Rookies, one of the best things you can do is get with a veteran, let him show you the ropes.' Everybody was scared as hell of Adrian Dantley," Malone said. "The first day of camp, he was looking at me and I was looking at him. We didn't have a confrontation, but maybe I fouled him a little hard."

Eventually, Dantley took Malone under his wings, providing him with scouting reports on players, refs, coaches and reporters.

But he didn't stop there, which is why Layden traded Dantley to the Detroit Pistons for Kelly Tripucka.

"Dantley was poison," Layden said. "We had to get him away from Karl. He was telling Karl he shouldn't go all out all the time, stuff like that. That's the reason for the trade."

Malone was stunned.

"I'm saying to myself, 'What in the hell are the Jazz doing,'" Malone told *Playboy*. "Who do they think is gonna score? Who's going to lead the team now?' "

Hey, Karl, *guess* who?

"Coach Layden called me and said, 'Oh, Karl, we got rid of Adrian.' "

"Yeah?"

"You know what that means?"

"Nope."

"You've got to play that much harder."

"I said, 'I am playing hard.' "

"You have to want that other rebound, you have to score with that last shot. You have to pick up your game a level."

Layden had tagged him as Utah's new go-to-guy, but Malone wanted him to go in a different direction.

That infuriated Layden.

"Karl, can you do it or not?" Layden asked. "If not, we'll get somebody else to do it."

At that point, Malone got down to the business of getting down to business, which is the hardest job of all.

Great players usually have great work ethics.

During his first years in Milwaukee, for example, Kareem Abdul-Jabbar ran every morning around dawn, and routinely won the Bucks' pre-season 400-meter dashes. Later, he lifted weights fanatically and trained under karate master Bruce Lee. As part of his intellectual zest, he also studied the philosophy of 17th century samurai warrior Miyamoto Musashi.

Malone, for his part, made the weight room his second home. In 1986 he built a weight room in his own home in Salt Lake City's tony Federal Heights section. It contained $100,000 worth of equipment as well as personal memorabilia, including his high school letter jacket, which looks absurdly small now.

"That's why I have it where I have it," he told *Sport.* "Right by my weight room."

The letter jacket is a reminder of how far Malone has come - and how hard he needs to push himself still. Even now, Malone lifts free weights three times a week during the off-season and twice a week during the season.

In the summer, on the farm, Malone goes into overdrive.

"He bales hay, fixes fence, and runs the Caterpillar grader to clear forest," John, his uncle, told the *Salt Lake City Tribune.*

After that, Malone runs up to 10 miles per day at a nearby track, then heads to his weight room – a re-modeled garage – and works his way through barbells, leg presses, bench presses, lifting machines, treadmills and stationary bikes.

"Karl can push more iron with his arms and legs than most people can with a Caterpillar," his Uncle John said.

Malone is fanatical about summer conditioning because he knows most players aren't.

"It's important to me mentally and physically," he told *The Sporting News.* "Mentally, I realize what summer means to 90 percent of the players. What summer means to them is vacation – meaning they do absolutely nothing until maybe a month before the season starts. That's my rallying time.

"Everyone wants something to rally around, and that's mine – working harder than other people in summertime. There are times I'd rather be hunting and fishing, but I get up and spend that time training."

Malone has become a mentor to Miami Heat center Isaac Austin, who was cut by the Jazz, bounced around Europe and the CBA, and then won the NBA's 1997 Most Improved Player Award.

Austin tried to keep pace with Malone during a summer visit, but by dinnertime, after all the running and lifting, he was ready for some downtime.

"When I got back from lifting, I just fell asleep, right there on the table," Austin said. "Everybody was laughing, and Karl was like, well, 'Man, just go to your room.'

"You've got to understand, Karl wasn't given everything on a silver platter. Karl worked hard for everything he got and he knew it took hard work for him to get where he is, so why give up now?"

During the tag-end of the 97-98 regular season, Coach Jerry Sloan gave the team a day off following an exhausting 10-game, 17-day road trip.

Malone was up at dawn the next morning, pumping iron.

"I've never seen Karl tired," Stockton told *Sports Illustrated* in 1988. "He's on a different standard than the rest of us."

"Jordan doesn't get tired. Bird doesn't. The great ones don't," added Frank Layden. "Karl wishes there were 200 games a year. He gets stronger as the year goes on. He thrives on playing."

Denver Nuggets coach Bill Hanzlik was in Salt Lake City with his young team in the summer of 1997 when he saw Malone working out in a downtown health club.

It was a Sunday morning.

"I told him how much I respected him, back when I was playing, and still today," Hanzlik said.

As he was leaving, Hanzlik wished his team had seen Malone as well.

"I said to heck with this and woke up the players and brought them over," said Hanzlik, who found Malone teaching an aerobics class when he returned with his players.

"Karl was in the middle of a spin class, dripping sweat, soaking wet. The rookies stood there for 15 minutes just watching him."

When Malone finished, he delivered a little sermon to Hanzlik's players.

"He talked for 15 minutes about our work ethic, how you have to devote your life to basketball," Hanzlik said.

"Off the court there are things like your family, and you've got to have that, but you can't be caught up in entourages and things like that.

"That one meeting was worth more than the whole 10 days we spent in summer camp."

Malone wasn't as kind to his own teammates when he reported for pre-season camp. In fact, when he saw Greg Ostertag's ring of flab, he blew a gasket.

"There's no doubt in my mind that if Greg Ostertag spent some more time on conditioning, his game would come around and he could be an all-star player," Malone told *The Sporting News*. "I take a lot of heat for criticizing his work ethic, but I want what's best for Karl Malone.

"My career has been made; his hasn't. I guess what I hate is wasted talent. When God gives you something, you should try to get the most out of it. I see an all-star right in front of me in that kid. I just wished he wanted it for himself as bad as I want it for him."

Malone, meanwhile, opened camp with a career-low 4 percent body fat and a few pounds short of his normal playing weight.

"I want to be as good or better than I was last year," he said. "That's what's driving me."

THE KARL MALONE CONTINUING EDUCATION PROJECT didn't end in the weight room.

He made only 48% of his free throws and had limited shooting range in his rookie year, and both problems were career-threatening.

"The guy couldn't even hit the backboard on free throws and I was furious," Layden said.

If a player can't sink a free throw, he's useless in the final quarter, because opponents will send him to the line time after time. A bad shooter is less apt to play aggressively on offense, which is especially costly for a power forward, whose game depends on aggression.

"And it can spread to the rest of the team," veteran point guard Mark Price said. "If a guy misses 3-4-5 in a row, the other guys start asking, 'What if I miss?' So now, you have another person."

The real damage, however, is more basic.

"For a player, nothing is more embarrassing than missing a shot at the end of the game or shooting an air ball," ex-Nuggets assistant coach Doug Moe Jr. said. "It's choking – and in sports, that's considered the ultimate sin. It's horrible to go to the line when you have no feel, no confidence. You've got 17,000 fans all around you. You feel everyone is watching you, watching your every move."

Added Price: "That's why it's so interesting to watch guys at the end of games. Some just fade; they don't want the ball. They don't want to have to shoot a free throw with everything at stake, especially when you're one point behind and you've got a chance to tie and win."

Charley Rosen, formerly a CBA coach, knows of that fear.

"When you're missing," he said, "the basket spits at the ball: 'Get that ugly thing out of here.' "

A lot of NBA players feel as if they have spit on their faces. Wilt Chamberlain led the NBA in field-goal percentage nine times. But from the line, he was a mess. He made less than half his attempts during six seasons. In 1971-72, he made only 42%. He went 0-for-10 one night and 0-for-9 another.

To end his woes, Chamberlain shot from the "elbow" where the free throw line intersects the circle, tried a jump shot and a two-handed underhand shot. Nothing worked.

Layden called on all his tricks to help Malone at the free-throw line.

One day he threw a dollar bill on the floor. He told the Jazz: If they sink two in a row, they pick up the dollar. If they don't, the whole team runs a couple wind sprints.

A sophomoric trick?

Maybe, but it worked, eventually.

"For a few years there, I was the worst coach in the NBA," Layden said after winning Coach-of-the-Year honors in '84. "Not only that, I was also the worst dressed, the sloppiest, the fattest and all that. Listen, our boosters club? By the end of the season, they'd turned into a terrorist group. Then, suddenly, like overnight I became a sleeping intellectual. People started to ask me my opinions on politics, religion and there was a little talk of running me for Utah governor. Isn't it interesting how smart I got in one season?"

But Layden was just beginning his work with Malone,

whose shooting from the field matched his futility from the line.

Not that shooting is an easy art. Hand a ball to a good athlete who has never shot a jumper and watch him. It isn't a pretty sight.

Peter Brancazio, a physics professor at Brooklyn College, calculated the amount of energy required in the shot-put, a slap-shot in hockey, pitching a baseball and shooting a 15-foot jumper. He measured each in joules, a metric unit of energy use.

The number of joules increases with the amount of force required. In other words, the difference between throwing a 10-pound stone and a one-pound stone would be reflected in the number of joules.

In all, a 15-footer jumper requires 15 joules, compared to 680 for the shot-put, 170 for a slap-shot and 120 for a pitch.

The average shooter puts about five pounds of force on the ball, Brancazio figures, and the difference between hitting the front and the back of the rim is only one and one-half to two ounces.

The point: More things can go wrong more often for a shooter.

Nevertheless, after years of tedious practice, Malone mastered this arcane art. He now makes 75% of his free throws and has developed a lethal fall-away jumper from 20 feet.

In his second season, Malone also began to master the game-within-the-game as well.

"I felt the referees out more and more," he said. "Now I know, when the ball is shot, if they're going to let me push the guy in the back to get the rebound. I know if I'm going to be able to grab a guy by the jersey when the referee is not looking and then get out on the break quick.

"I know I'm going to be able to step on a guy's feet where he's trying to shoot; I know the referee is not looking at players' feet. The guy hasn't jumped, but they don't know why. Or if I get ready to shoot, I would act like I was shooting, but I'd really be trying to hit my man in the face with my elbow. Not dirty, but just seeing what I could get away with."

Added Malone: "And I might hit a guy harder coming across the lane, for no reason."

In his second season, Malone averaged 21.7 points and 10 rebounds per game, and served notice of dream seasons to come.

Nevertheless, he was summoned to coach Frank Layden's office once more.

"That was a great job. Now, over the summer, I want you to work on running the floor more. I want you to work on your outside shot. I want you to work on coming inside more. I want you to work on your free throws," Layden said after the Mailman's second season.

"Is that all?" Malone chuckled.

From Layden, the Mailman learned what was expected.

In 1988, despite his success, Layden retired, abruptly, citing burnt-out, his 350-pound girth, disrespect from fans and refs, and the incessant travel. When ref John Madden tossed him from a game, the weary coach said he had had enough.

"As I sat there, I thought, 'What was that?' I'm a professional, a former coach of the year, at the top of my profession, and this guy just lowered me to the lowest level," said Layden, who came back in 1998 to coach the Utah Starzz of the WNBA. "He embrassed me, stepped on me like I was dirt. That's when I realized, this isn't fun. I was never the same after that."

In 1997, as Malone prepared for his 13th NBA season, Nuggets rookie Danny Fortson asked him: "How did you get so good from your rookie season to the next?"

It was the ultimate tribute to Malone's first NBA coach.

Chapter Four

The Ultimate Duo

The art of being a great point guard consists to a large extent of knowing exactly when to stop, and going a bit farther.

John Stockton instinctively realizes that, which is why he mobilized himself for action on the morning of the game he passed Oscar Robertson to move into second place on the NBA's all-time assists list.

As he entered the Delta Center in Salt Lake City, Stockton's quick-darting eyes immediately fastened on the upper balcony, which was draped with banners in his honor.

Stockton, to whom all public attention and self-promotion are a torture, was peeved by this display of unseemly hype.

"Get 'em outta here," he told a club official.

The Jazz told him to take a hike, which might have

been the first time Stockton was humbled on his home court.

Selflessness is an uncommon virtue in the 90s, as are point guards who'd rather pass than shoot, which makes Stockton a rare and enigmatic star.

In an era when conspicuousness passes for distinction, he still reveres hard-nosed defense and seamless team-work; still hits game-winning shots with little ado; still prefers small-town reserve to cosmopolitan excess and still plays on and on, night after night.

Like Karl Malone.

"They're superstars who are down home," forward Antoine Carr said in *Stockton to Malone! The Rise of the Utah Jazz.* "I mean, I've run across a lot of guys in this league who thought they were better than everybody else and kind of carried themselves that way. But these guys are normal guys. They like to go fishing, hunting. They hang out together, do those things together. I've never really seen superstars like that."

Malone and Stockton are not only on the same page; they wrote the user's manual on symbiotic relationships and basketball.

Malone is the primary reason Stockton is one of the greatest passers in NBA history. Stockton is the primary reason Malone is a remarkable scorer and rebounder and the greatest power forward ever.

Both have been All-Star game MVPs; both were selected to the NBA's 50th Anniversary team, both are bound for the Hall of Fame.

In 1995, Stockton passed Magic Johnson to become No. 1 on the all-time assists list; in 1996 he became the all-time steals leader.

In 1997, Malone became the oldest player ever to win the MVP Trophy.

In every poll, they rank with West-Baylor, Magic-Kareem, Oscar-Lucas, Cousy-Russell and Jordan-Pippen on the list of greatest duos in hoop history.

In fact, Malone and Stockton have forged a relationship that might never again be seen in the NBA, now that free agents rush en masse to the highest bidders.

"Every night when they go to bed, John should say, 'Thank you Karl' and Karl should say, 'Thank you John,' " Frank Layden said. "They're Tinker to Evans, and Montana to Rice.

"This place was perfect for them, a small town, a small community. Who knows? Had they gone to New York or Los Angeles, maybe it would have been different. Here, they blended, they grew, they got better."

Added Jazz announcer Hot Rod Hundley: "Stockton and Malone operate like they're on one wavelength. Basketball requires split-second timing. They have a relationship no one else can fill. I've watched the game all my life and played against the best players and seen the best, and I've never seen two players play as well together as those two."

That was never more evident than in Game Four of the 1997 NBA Championships. The Chicago Bulls led 73-72 with less than a minute left, Michael Jordan had just missed a long range-jumper, and Stockton scrambled inside to grab the defensive rebound.

Glancing up-court, he saw two flashes - Malone and Jordan - then transformed himself into Steve Young, throwing a perfect 80-foot strike to Malone, who laid it in for the winner.

It seemed only fitting: The NBA's greatest passer wins the game with a pass, not a shot.

"That's the pass that I'll remember out of all the great ones he's made. It had to be perfect," Malone said.

Stockton and Malone's telepathic instincts are just as evident when Stockton is leading the break and the Mailman is trailing. As he streaks toward the hoop, scanning the court like a mobile radar, Stockton is apt to leap, look to another teammate, and then flip a blind backward pass over his shoulder to Malone, who is preparing for the spot-up jumper.

"Some of the things they do, they can do blindfolded," Los Angeles Lakers coach Del Harris said.

Take the pick and roll for example. It's the oldest play in the book, but Stockton and Malone run it as though they wrote the book. Even when opponents know it's coming, they're usually incapable of delaying, much less stopping it.

In fact, it's the NBA's version of the Green Bay Packer power sweep. It's also a symbol of their no-frills grit.

"Neither of them will ever be late for a bus, a practice, or a game," forward Adam Keefe added. "Neither of them will ever cut corners in practice.

"They're not concerned with how they're seen in the big picture, if they drive the nicest cars or have the most flamboyant clothing. That doesn't appeal to them. What appeals to them are the basics of life - and winning."

In many ways, Stockton and Salt Lake City are an ideal fit. Jazz fans admire his humility, emotional reserve and invulnerable passion for victory. To Stockton, Salt Lake City is Spokane writ large.

"I'll never know what any other team or NBA city would have been like - and I don't want to find out," Stockton said. "I can't think of a better team to be part of or a better home than Salt Lake City to raise your kids. Those are things you can't put a value on."

Nevertheless, when the Jazz made him the 16th pick of the 1984 NBA Draft, fans bellowed their disapproval. "A wimp," went the common refrain.

"At the Salt Palace, we had a stage set up," Scott Layden said. "We had a few hundred people, diehard, sicko basketball nuts in to watch the draft, and we gave out free Cokes and hot dogs and stuff. It came time for the 16th pick and my dad said to Sam Battistone, who was the owner, 'Why don't you go up and announce who the pick is this year?'

"Sam walked to the podium. He said, 'The Jazz draft 6-1 point guard from Gonzaga, John Stockton.' As 'Stockton' came out of his mouth, the hot dogs came flying, the Coke cups, the people were booing. Sam turned around, came back to my dad, and said, 'Well, thanks a lot. Now I know why you wanted me to do it.'

The fans thought we drafted Dick Stockton." (This was meant as a joke, referring to the NBA broadcaster.)

Jazz announcer Hot Rod Hundley interviewed Stockton on a conference call immediately afterward.

"Is everybody booing?" Stockton asked Hundley.

"No, they're not saying, 'Boo,' " said Hundley. "They're saying, 'Who?' "

Frank and Scott Layden anticipated an outpouring of criticism. After all, Gonzaga flies below most fans' radar, and Stockton looks more like a stockbroker than a record-breaker.

But the Laydens knew about Stockton's huge hands, long fingers and extraordinary peripheral vision, which reminded them of Bob Cousy, whose ball-handling wizardry had changed the game a quarter-century before.

They knew about his determination. "He'd run face-first into a brick wall at full speed if he had to," an ex-coach said.

They knew about his hyper-competitiveness.

"He holds the Jazz record on the treadmill, and he wants to defend that title every year," said Jeff Condill, a college teammate.

They knew about his intelligence.

"The smartest player I've ever seen," Malone said.

And they knew he was a throwback to another era, when point guards were ball distributors, not point accumulators.

"Nobody can distribute the ball plus lead his team like John Stockton," said Magic Johnson, whose career assists record was broken by the Jazz point man. "His whole thing is to get everybody involved."

Frank Layden also knew about Stockman's roots in the Roman Catholic working-class section of Spokane, which reminded him of his early years in Brooklyn.

"He has a lot of things going for him. He's Irish, he's Catholic, he laughs at my jokes and his dad owns a bar," Layden quipped.

Spokane's Little Vatican section has produced plenty of policemen and priests, and a luminary or two, including Bing Crosby, who no doubt considered his roots while playing priests in *Going My Way* and *The Bells of St. Mary's*.

Stockton's father's tavern, which opened ten days before John's birth, is within short walking distance of their home, which is a short walk from the grammar and high schools John attended, which are a short walk from Gonzaga University, where John would eventually attract the attention of the Utah Jazz.

Stockton has never abandoned his roots; after signing his first NBA contract, he bought the house next to his parents' and married his college sweetheart.

"He's as steady as a ticktock of a clock," Malone said.

Sports course through the Stocktons' blood. Houston Stockton, John's grandfather, was an all-American halfback at Gonzaga and a professional star.

After flirting with football and baseball, John focused on basketball with a compulsive drive that is common among basketball stars with common gifts.

Chris Mullin was a classic gym rat. He played round the clock, and along with friends, often sneaked into the gym at St. Thomas Aquinas grammar school. Once, during a blizzard, they spent the entire weekend there, sleeping in the coaches' office and eating in the trainer's room. It was Chris' definition of a heavenly experience.

At St. John's, his practice rituals were legendary. Coach Lou Carnesecca recalls an incident after Mullin's junior year, when he'd been named to the Olympic team.

"The night before the final cuts for the Olympic team, I remembered I'd forgotten to wish Mul luck," he said in *The Golden Boys*. "It was about ten at night and I said, 'I bet you he's in the gym.' I went up to the gym, the lights are on, and who the hell do you think is in the gym? "

In 1987, after a stay at a re-hab center for alcoholics, the gym became Mullin's ultimate safe haven.

"The legendary workouts began," Cameron Stauth wrote in *The Golden Boys*. "Six to seven hours a day. Suicide drills. Long-distance running. Thousands of sit-ups. Shooting for hours with a weight vest on. Pumping iron. Balance work. Shooting 360 jumpers per half hour, and making ninety percent of them. Shooting 100 three-pointers with the weight vest on and making 80 percent. Shooting free throws with the vest, and making up to 190 in a row."

Larry Bird was just as obsessed.

"I would play at 6 a.m. before school. I'd duck into the gym in between classes to get up a few shots and play again after school into the early hours of the next morning, feeling that sleep was a rude intrusion on my practice time," he wrote in *Drive*.

Chris Jackson, who later changed his name to Mahmoud Abdul-Rauf, remains a legend in Gulfport, La., for his aesthetic discipline. As a young boy, he dribbled a basketball while riding his bike to a nearby court, practiced until dusk, then dribbled a basketball while riding his bike home.

His mother grew increasingly concerned about her son's monomania.

"I would ask him, 'You've done it all day, why don't you stop? Why can't you just do it for seven hours, and then quit? Why do you do this day after day?' I'd never heard of anybody spending so much time playing basketball. It scared me a little bit."

Bert Jenkins, his high school coach, was taken aback as well.

"In my 40 years of coaching, I've never seen anyone practice so hard, so much," he said in 1990, after the Denver Nuggets had drafted the LSU star with the third pick.

"He isn't the best natural talent. Even in high school, we had stronger kids, faster kids, quicker kids. But his skill development was unbelievable. He was the ultimate gym rat. He never was a kid with lots of means. When other kids were going to the movies, he was going to play ball. He's not a loner; he's just all business. But for him, it's not work, it's fun. Basketball makes him happy, and he wants to be perfect at the thing that makes him happiest.

"I've seen him get so upset after missing a shot. I'll say, 'Even Magic and Larry Bird miss shots.' But any kind of mistake bothers him deeply. Sometimes I wish he'd loosen up, and, say, shoot a hook from halfcourt. You know take a crazy shot just to have fun."

Jenkins' players shot free throws before each practice, but he had to junk that policy because of Jackson, who practices his shooting with Zen-like persistence.

"One day Chris made 283 in a row," he said. "We couldn't start practice for 45 minutes. A few weeks later he hit 267 in row. And then 243. He was destroying our practices. One player put his head on the ball and said, 'Wake me when it's over.'"

Stockton played round the clock as well, often against his brother, Steve. The Stockton brothers were nicknamed Cain and Abel because of their furious one-on-one games in the family driveway, located within hailing distance of a convent for retired nuns.

"In the summer, we'd play forever," Steve told *The Sporting News*. "And John was gaining on me. So I go up for a shot and he elbows me, splits my lip all the way across. At the first chance, I gave him an elbow back, the first time he leaves his stomach unprotected. He ran to the house and was crying from the porch, and then he starts yelling every profanity known to man."

The nuns across the alley slammed their windows shut, but a few hours later the Stockton boys were at it again.

When his grade-school coach announced the school

gym would open at 6 a.m. on summer days, he didn't expect any takers. But Stockton was at the front door, every morning at 6 sharp.

At the public courts, he would stand around until the older kids tired and finally picked him.

In *The Golden Boys*, Stockton's high school coach, Ed Smith, remembers Stockton's daily calls for pickup games, the conversation beginning like this: " 'Open the gym and bring your fat friends.' What were we? Twenty-four, twenty-five? It wasn't like we were forty-five. These guys had played. John was a five-five ninth grader. He'd play his butt off and get mad if he got beat by a 25-year-old. Tons of players were as gifted as he was, but he had something other people don't. Many would call that 'something' desire, but I'm not sure that word adequately covers it."

Fear also drove Stockton. Stacy, his older sister, once heard him praying in the shower. His plea: Please help me grow as tall as the sliding glass door (6-feet).

"In the shower, you have time to think," said Stockton, who ended up 6-1.

Stockton looked like a sophomore his senior year at Gonzaga Prep, which is why he received only passing interest from major colleges in the region.

"Don't think that didn't scare some recruiters away," Dan Fitzgerald, Stockton's college coach, told *Sports Illustrated*. "(Washington State's) George Raveling didn't come after John and later admitted it was the biggest recruiting mistake he ever made."

Stockton's worth rose season-by-season at Gonzaga, along with his cockiness. "While visiting L.A. in college, he'd walked up to Bernadette Peters in an airport lounge and invited her to a game," Stauth wrote in *The Golden Boys*.

"Then he had come back and told his teammates that he was taking her out that night. Also while he was in college, Gonzaga's sports information department had distributed a weekly newsletter called the *Stock Report*, pushing him (unsuccessfully) for All-American honors. On the first day of NBA rookie camp, he wrote his college coach that 'It's a lot of fun playing with so many great players. They aren't awesome, though. I feel confidence playing against them.' "

At the 1984 Olympic Trials, Stockton was among the last players cut by coach Bobby Knight, but not before thoroughly distinguishing himself, which only increased his confidence.

"Deep inside he knew he was as good as most of the players there. It was like a springboard," Steve said.

Nevertheless, because of his slight stature and no-frills style - and the fact he's Caucasian - Stockton was perceived as an over-achiever with underwhelming talent.

"Some people say, 'Hey, I could be like John Stockton, he isn't too big or too strong.' Well that's garbage," Fitzgerald said. "You can't imagine how many letters I get from the parents of 5-foot-10 Caucasian point guards telling me their son is the next John Stockton and I say, 'Bull....A guy like this comes around once every 10 years.' "

Added Malone: "Other (point guards) come into the league and they've got the flashy moves and the endorsements. Then they come play against John and he teaches them that you can play this game without putting the ball between your legs 20 times before you do something with it."

At the NBA's pre-draft camp in Chicago in 1984, Scott Layden realized the magnitude of Stockton's skills by the way he obscured his teammates' limitations.

"He made Kevin Willis look like a real player," he said. "Kevin really owes Stockton. He doesn't know it, but he should give part of his paycheck to Stockton. Willis was running down the court, dunking the ball. Stockton was dishing it to him, and if I remember back, Willis almost looked like Karl Malone."

During Stockton's early Jazz days, he went to extraordinary lengths to protect his privacy. He remained in the trainer's room after games until deadline-pressured media members departed for their computers. Then he'd slip out a side exit to avoid autograph-seekers.

Even in Spokane, a down-home city of 180,000, Stockton shields himself off from attention off-court.

When *Sports Illustrated* did a long feature piece on Mark Rypien, Ryne Sandberg and Stockton - all Spokane residents - Stockton refused to participate, even though the article was implicitly favorable.

And in his father's bar, Jack and Dan's Tavern, posters of John are quickly removed if anyone is brazen enough to tack them up.

"I tell people John never put a shift behind the bar, so if anybody's picture goes up, it ought to be mine or my partners," Jack told *The Sporting News.* "You know once I think John put some up, but I took them down. I don't want to exploit his fame. I think it's just too much braggadocio."

In fact, Stockton has struggled to live a simple, understated life, mirroring his playing style.

One of his hobbies is flying, and in the summer of 1996, a pilot with the Air Force Thunderbirds allowed him to briefly take over control of an F-16 jet. While describing the feeling to *Sports Illustrated,* Stockton revealed his inner workings.

"They're normal guys outside the plane, but inside they're pretty special," he said. "When you watch them, you realize it takes only the slightest touch to do some amazing things. It's like everything else, I guess. When you get guys who are the best in the world at what they do, they make it look easy."

In 1996, while negotiating a three-year, $15 million deal, this father of four demanded a clause protecting his freedom to roughhouse with his children. That was unprecedented in the NBA, where special clauses usually cover more exotic endeavors.

"There are wonderful qualities he has," Frank Layden said. "We've got to use John as an example of what the right thing is. Unfortunately, he's quiet and unavailable. So we lose some of that. Most of the players in the league are good guys. But who gets the ink? The bad guys. We've got to tell people: 'Be like John Stockton. It pays off.' "

The Stockton pick paid off for the Jazz from day one. He was a backup to Rickey Green during his rookie season, yet set team records for steals (109) and assists (415). He was Green's backup the following season as well, but averaged 23.6 minutes per game compared to 18.2 the previous season.

More importantly, this was Malone's rookie season, and the writing was on every wall.

"Never has the NBA had two teammates of this stature whose brilliant careers were so intertwined," wrote pro basketball writer Terry Pluto.

"Stockton is the Bob Cousy of his era, the point guard with tremendous vision and huge hands who can deliver a pass right off the dribble. Malone is the classic power forward, a man who brought muscle and size into the league and developed grace."

Stockton became the starter in the '86-87 season and records began to fall. During the fading days of the regular season he had 16 assists against Golden State and 20 against Cleveland the next night, pushing him over the 1,000 barrier for the season. Only two other players in NBA history - Detroit's Isiah Thomas (1,123, 1984-85) and Kevin Porter (1,099, 1978-79) - had accomplished that.

During the '87-88 season, he averaged an astonishing 13.8 assists per game and broke the NBA single-season mark with a total of 1,128. He also finished third in the NBA in steals (2.95 per game) and fourth in field-goal percentage (.574), and earned all-NBA second-team honors aside his best buddy.

"Anything I can do in life that can be with Karl Malone, I'm thrilled by. The more things we can share as we're playing - and after - the better for me," said Stockton, who opened an auto dealership with Malone in Sandy, Utah, in the mid 90s.

Added the Mailman: "I spend a lot of time with Stockton, although it's one of those things we don't talk about a lot. In this day and age, with professional athletes and grown men, it's one of those things people think is corny. For men to be close like we are."

The Stockton-Malone connection delivered the Jazz to a franchise record 47-35 record in '87-88 and into the Western Conference semifinals against the Los Angeles Lakers.

The following season Karl Malone won MVP honors at the All-Star game - Stockton was runner-up - and the Jazz finished with a 51-31 record and the Midwest Division title.

On and on it went. Nineteen-ninety-two was the Dream Team year.

In 1993, Malone and Stockton were Co-MVPs of the All-Star game, played at the Delta Center.

In 1996, they were both selected to the list of the 50 Greatest Players in NBA history.

They needed one another; as the Jazz' leading men continued to attract world-wide attention, critics continued to mount attacks over their inability to win a title, or, prior to 1996, even advance to the NBA finals.

Stockton also came under increasing fire for dirty play.

"To me, he's one of the dirtiest players in the league," said former Detroit Pistons center Scott Hastings. "He's the Danny Ainge of the 90s, without the reputation. I'm watching Stockton on some game film the other day, and he turns around and beats the hell out of David Robinson, drills him into the ground. A scuffle starts, and during the scuffle he's not involved in it, he goes to officials and starts complaining. And then all of a sudden he starts getting calls."

The way Stockton sees it, he's just defending his turf and protecting his 6-foot-1 175-pound body from the7-foot plus Robinson, one of the league's giants.

"You have to stand your ground," he said. "Contact is part of it, and I don't mind contact.

"One guy, Scott Hastings, said I was a dirty player, but I'll tell you, if I'm a dirty player, there's a long list of guys ahead of me. I could talk about my game until I was blue in the face and it wouldn't make a difference."

Stockton's smaller-than-life size as well as his letter-sweater looks contribute to his mischief-making, many say, because he uses it to simultaneously rile opponents and pacify officials.

"He actually initiates a lot of it," former Nuggets Assistant Coach Mike Evans said. "He tends to get the call, but he's actually starting it. And he's never committed a foul."

Malone bristles at the suggestions Stockton - the NBA's

No. 1 pick-setter pound-for-pound - is a deliberately malicious player.

"I worry about John down there, getting whacked around by the guys who guard me," Malone said. "I draw all kinds of defenders, from the big quick guys like David Robinson to the power guys like Charles Oakley. John takes 'em all on.

"And you have guys who were jealous because he made the Olympic team, because he led the league in assists. There's a lot of animosity in this league, but John is amazing because if you look at head-to-head competition, he's there. Consistently."

Another question dogged Malone and Stockton as well: How good would one be without the other?

"I don't even want to think about it," Malone said.

The Mailman didn't have to during his first 12 years. Entering the 1997-98 season, he and Stockton had missed just four games apiece in 25 combined seasons.

"What they've done is equivalent to Cal Ripken. I don't mean to be disrespectful of baseball, but it's easier to play shortstop than to play in the NBA," Frank Layden said.

But Stockton's long run came to a painful end shortly before the start of the 1997-98 season, when he underwent knee surgery and was forced to miss the first 18 games.

At that point, Stockton had played in 1,062 regular-season games, 127 playoff contests, two Olympics, nine all-star games, more than 100 exhibition games and thousands of practices.

Malone, meanwhile, had really never played without his partner. Could he flourish without Stockton?

After leading the team to 11 wins while contributing his usual quota of points, rebounds and impassioned leadership, the answer seemed obvious.

"He's still great and just as strong," TV analyst Rolando Blackman said.

So was Stockton when he returned to the lineup for the 19th game of the season.

Perhaps the Stockton-Malone connection clicked best in the 1996-97 playoffs.

In Game Six of the Western Conference Championship Series against the Houston Rockets, with the score tied at 100, coach Jerry Sloan called for a pick and roll, the staple.

With 2.8 seconds left Bryon Russell inbounded the ball to Stockton - a split-second after Malone had thrown his massive body in front of Clyde Drexler. That's a little bit like a defensive tackle throwing his body in front of a punter.

Drexler couldn't begin to get around Malone, Charles Barkley couldn't make the switch, Stockton received the pass, then buried the three-pointer that lifted the Jazz into their first championship series.

"Great pick," the laconic Sloan said afterwards.

Others were more expressive:

"Karl Malone has been setting picks to free John Stockton for a dozen years, and he set one last night that freed an entire franchise," wrote Bob Ford of the *Philadelphia Inquirer*. "There couldn't be a more fitting finish to Utah's endless quest for an NBA championship round than a Malone pick to give Stockton an open shot."

Ten days later, Stockton threw the bomb heard round the basketball world, the long pass over the top of Jordan's head to Malone, who laid in the winner in Game Four against the Bulls at the Delta Center.

"For a dozen years the Jazz has watched in wonder as John Stockton has fed Karl Malone for big buckets," wrote Andrew Bagnato of the *Chicago Tribune*. "But on Sunday they hooked-up for their biggest ever. On the score sheet, it went down as 'K. Malone FB Layup (J. Stockton).'

"In the Utah history book, it will go down as the moment that the Jazz declared itself legitimate contenders to the Bulls' throne, the moment that these two old teammates and friends lifted the Jazz to a thrilling 78-73 win over the Bulls ...The Pittsburgh Steelers had the 'Immaculate Reception' by Franco Harris. The San Francisco 49ers had 'The Catch' by Dwight Clark. And now the Utah jazz has 'The Pass.' "

But Malone and Stockton won't rest until they win an NBA Championship. They're incapable of less.

"We don't want to leave this game owing anything," Malone said. "We want to be able to say that we gave the game of basketball everything we had, and in return the game gave us everything. We're even. Because that's how we came into this league and that's how we want to go out.

"If Stockton and I happen to go to the Hall of Fame, I'm sure they'll try to work in both our schedules that we're there at the same time because we're bonded together for life. I couldn't think of a better guy to be bonded with."

Chapter Five

Enforcer Extraordinaire

Since 1985, the NBA has witnessed some memorable shots from Karl Malone.

He knocked David Robinson unconscious with a devastating elbow, bloodied Isiah Thomas' face, floored Sidney Moncrief, flattened Charles Outlaw.

The hit parade goes on and on, like a January road trip, reinforcing Malone's image as an enforcer extraordinaire.

Off the court, Malone is a courtly giant . But on it, he's all brutal reality; ready, in an instant, to deal with a welter of threats with a wealth of overpowering weapons.

"I'm a country boy who enjoys a dogfight," he said.

The fight isn't always physical. The Mailman also uses his tongue, which doubles as a carving knife, to lacerate targets, especially Generation X's sullen stars.

Not surprisingly, Malone is often isolated in controversy.

"Some guys in the NBA (don't like me). But you know what? That doesn't bother me," he said. "Do you know what that does for me? It makes me play harder. I don't have to impress them. I don't care if you think I'm a horse's behind. I was never their friend and I'm not out there to make friends.

"I've always been the kind of guy who's danced to his own music. If you don't like me, you don't like me. But I'm going to please Karl Malone."

Malone's warrior ways have endeared him to another enforcer, Mike Tyson.

During a 1988 party for Magic Johnson, Iron Mike entered the room, nodded curtly to other stars and then made his way to the awe-struck Malone.

"Yo, Mailman," the heavyweight champ intoned. "I want to talk to you."

Malone quickly stood.

Tyson smiled.

"You're my man, Mailman," he said.

Malone was a man-child when he entered the NBA, but it didn't take him long to learn the ways and wiles of its most fearsome men. In fact, he laid down the tracks for his future during an edgy showdown with Maurice Lucas.

During the 70s and early 80s, Lucas intimidated nearly everyone.

During a referee strike, a substitute official started to call a foul on him. Just as he prepared to blow the whistle,

Lucas' hand touched the chain. Lucas shook his head slowly, his eyes cold with fury. "You don't want to do that," he said.

The ref slowly took the whistle out of his mouth and hurried downcourt.

In Lucas' early days, Hubie Brown took him out of a game, enraged with his uninspired play. The coach dressed him down before Lucas turned and headed toward the end of the bench to avoid further humiliation.

But Brown followed him, continuing his tirade. Finally the coach turned and returned to the team huddle.

A few moments later, Lucas grabbed Brown from behind, spun him around, and warned: "Don't ever do that again."

Lucas' baleful power first came to the fore against 7-foot-2 Artis Gilmore after the brawny center had chased him downcourt.

After catching his tormentor at halfcourt, pausing dramatically, Gilmore slowly and methodically backed Lucas toward the free-throw line, then past the free-throw line, and into a corner. When Lucas reached the baseline, when the rookie's options were spent, when his turf and manliness were on the line, he reacted characteristically.

He decked Gilmore with two quick rights, watched the towering center crumple to the hardwood and then danced around his first victim.

"You want some of me, big fella, you can come after me," he screamed at Gilmore, who never played the same again, many said.

In 1985, no one had to brief Karl Malone about Lucas, who played for the Los Angeles Lakers that season. And no one had to tell him that rookies who cower in the face of violence lose face. A confrontation with Lucas was inevitable, and Malone was armed and ready.

"Stop going over me," Lucas grumbled as they jostled for inside position, "before I hurt you."

Malone didn't bother to reply.

Instead, on Utah's next possession, he thundered downcourt like a steam train, went airborne and then shattered Lucas' composure with a devastating dunk that reverberated throughout the league.

"No one intimidates me," he screamed at Lucas.

No one doubted that, least of all Dominique Wilkins, who, after seeing a teammate fall prey to Mailman's KO power, screamed:

"You're a cheap-shot artist; you're not a man. You always go out there to hurt somebody smaller than you."

Malone was dazed at Dominique's diatribe because superstars don't usually berate fellow superstars and because he felt victimized.

"I get a lot of abuse," Malone said. "The players on the other side hold me, scratch me, push me in the back, everything but undress me. It's always two or three guys ganging up on me. Some guys come into a game just to beat up on me. Sometimes I take it personally."

After reviewing videotape, NBA executive Rod Thorn decided not to fine Malone, who felt vindicated, although that didn't stop his angry critics from piling on.

"Sometimes they (physical players like Malone) may do things without knowing it," Seattle forward Derrick McKey said, "But other times they do it intentionally to intimidate you. They 're aware of what they're doing and guys can get hurt because of it."

Malone's rap sheet grew in December 1991 at the Delta Center. As Detroit's Isiah Thomas sliced toward the hoop, Malone deserted his man to stop the clever point guard. Both Dream Teamers went up cleanly, but Thomas came down with gash above his right eye - the result of an errant Malone elbow - which required 40 stitches.

This time the Mailman was fined $10,000, suspended for one game and extensively criticized once more. The fact he didn't dispute the fine convinced many he had intentionally struck Thomas.

"I don't care what anybody says; it was an accident," he said. "I never said I agreed with the penalty. But I took the fine like a man and went on with my life. Everything happens for a reason. Right after it, I called Isiah in San Antonio and everything was settled. He said, 'Karl, I know what kind of player you are. Don't worry about what people say.' "

But Thomas warned Malone about retaliation in his hometown of Chicago.

"He said, 'Karl, just be careful in Chicago. I have crazy friends there,' " Malone recalled.

Malone received special protection during the Jazz' annual Chicago stop one month later. A policeman rode on the team bus, and the bus driver used a circular route from the hotel to the arena. Then he drove up a little-used road between two fenced-off parking lots. The team entered Chicago Stadium through a back ramp. A security officer sat behind the Jazz bench during the game, and accompanied the Mailman from locker to courtside and back again.

"Now I know what the President feels like," Malone said.

During the 1998 championship series against the Bulls, *Deseret News* television columnist Scott Pierce wrote that Thomas, now working as an NBA analyst, had unfairly criticized Malone in retribution for their 1992 dispute.

Thomas promptly called Pierce.

"Have you ever heard me say one negative thing about Karl Malone or John Stockton?" Thomas asked Pierce. "I didn't say one word. When Karl Malone apologized to me, that was the end of it."

Pierce wrote: "Of course he has criticized both Malone and Stockton for their play. But that's his job. What's harder to accept is that Thomas rejects the idea that he has expressed any bias at all during the on-going NBA finals. Thomas insists he has no bias, but when describing a couple of replays, he correctly pointed out that Malone had elbowed Jordan in the head and that Foster had shoved Jordan - but he failed to mention that the same replay clearly showed Jordan smacking Jeff Hornacek in the head with the elbow."

Thomas was never popular with other superstars, who

regarded him as a selfish ego-tripper. Moreover, as president of the Players Association, he'd worked on behalf of rank-and-file players at the superstars' expense.

But David Robinson is generally respected, if not feared, so when Malone KO'd the San Antonio Spurs center with an elbow to the head, the Mailman really had a PR problem.

Robinson, unconscious for two minutes, spent the night in a hospital, which only stirred the molten pot.

"I was not trying to knock David off or nothing. I was trying to get position," Malone insisted. "I score a lot of baskets just turning and going. It was an unfortunate thing that happened. I went by (the hospital) after the game and talked to him and everything ...He said, 'Karl, these things happen.' "

Only hours earlier, Malone had been named winner of the Henry Iba Citizen Athlete Award, given annually to a prominent national star for good works.

In 24 hours, the Mailman had KO'd a Dream Team center and won a humanitarian award.

Just another day in Karl's World.

"Off the court, Karl is caring, giving, sensitive," sports psychologist Bruce Ogilvie told *Men's Health* magazine. "Once he puts on a jockstrap, he's arrogant, almost paranoid. It's a personality style that's enabled him to become one of the best scorers in the NBA.

"Both sides are compatible. Each can help him function better. Many successful people take on a dual personality to be effective."

Added Malone: "It's like Dr. Jekyll and Mr. Hyde. But both sides of us get along."

Some opponents prefer the Dr. Jekyll side.

"Other teams know that if they can get Malone angry, especially in the playoffs, they have a significant probability of winning," Ogilvie said. "Malone has inordinate pride, but he also has a low threshold of stress. He's so brittle, with such a heightened sensitivity to slights, that with two bad calls against him he may be too frustrated to function. He's just never learned to say 'So be it.'"

Sometimes Malone's teammates exploit the Dr. Jekyll side. In 1990, for example, they told him an opposing player had called him "overrated." Malone went and scored 52 points, unaware that the allegation was nonsense.

But Malone is a virtual peace-nik compared with basketbrawlers of the 50s and 60s, even though a 1996 *USA Today* poll of 301 players, coaches, trainers and general managers named him the second-dirtiest player, behind only Dennis Rodman.

Consider one John Brisker, who set an ABA record for meanness with the Pittsburgh Condors. Brisker's own teammates feared him. At one point, the club even hired a football player to restrain him.

It didn't take long for Brisker and the new hire to get in a shoving match. "I'm going to get my gun," the football player declared. "I'm going to get mine," Brisker shouted back. Practice was promptly canceled.

To deal with the Brisker problem, Dallas coach Tom Nissalke offered a $500 reward to the first player to deck him. Lenny Chappell, a reserve, yelled, "How about starting me?"

Nissalke agreed, thinking Chappell would show some restraint. Instead, as the ball went up on the game-opening center jump, Chappell floored him. No one saw the blow; all eyes were on the ball.

Indiana Pacer star Billy Knight has dark memories of Brisker as well.

"The first time I played a game against Brisker, he just turned around and busted me in the mouth," he recalled in *Loose Balls*. "I mean, for no reason he just punched me in the mouth and stood there waiting for me to do something about it. I didn't do anything. He scared me."

Brisker reportedly became a mercenary soldier after his playing days ended.

Warren Jabali was another member of the ABA's thugocracy.

"I played with Jabali later in his career in Kentucky and our whole team was scared to death of the guy because he was so mean," Dan Issel, former Colonel and Denver Nuggets center said. "We were in the dressing room once and we had a black rookie on our team, I can't remember the kid's name. Any way, Warren noticed the kid was wearing some cotton underwear. Jabali reached over and literally ripped the shorts right off the kid. Warren said: 'Don't you know that our ancestors had to pick this cotton. Get yourself some slick drawers.' "

Jabali met his match in the Virginia Squires' Neil Johnson. After Jabali had pushed him to the ground, Johnson rose, walked toward his tormentor, then floored him with a single punch. "Get up you... racist, so I can really kick your ass."

Added referee John Vanak: "In 28 years of officiating, it was the most devastating punch I'd ever seen on the court."

During the NBA's early years, violence was as routine as clunky centers. Every team hired enforcers, whose job was to injure those who tried to injure the star.

"I don't want to sound like I'm bragging, because I'm not, but back then the violence was much more intense," said Satch Sanders, who played for the Boston Celtics. "The purpose of a fight was to take a player out of the game.

"The Celtics and Syracuse used to brawl every game - every single game. There were always at least one or two fights. There were games against Philadelphia where both teams were out on the floor and two or three different fights were going on simultaneously.

"There were cases of guys running under people - to mess up their backs - so those guys were out for an entire series. If that went on today, guys like Michael Jordan would never have existed - because they would have never left the ground.

"The players today aren't trying to hurt anybody - they're just trying to get an advantage. The talk about intimidation is good reading - but nothing's there."

The first real abominable showman was Boston's Jungle Jim Loscutoff, who was the pride of Celtics coach Red Auerbach. Red is an apt name because practices and games under him routinely turned bloody. One afternoon, Bob Brannum broke a teammate's nose as the friendly enemies scrimmaged.

"Part of the game," shrugged Auerbach, who forbade socializing with opponents.

In the 1950s, rookie Frank Mahoney was competing with two veterans for the center's job - until the vets' shoving, pushing and savage elbows drained him of his will. Auerbach shrugged again. "Part of the game."

In the 50s and 60s, picks were set with one hand covering the face. In one game, Terry Dischinger was at the top of the key, and Loscutoff was guarding the man behind Dischinger. Dischinger was setting a pick on Loscutoff when Loscutoff slid in between them while following his man. As he did, Loscutoff threw a blow that shattered Dischinger's nose. Blood covered the court, not to mention Dischinger.

Auerbach, who once exchanged punches with St. Louis Hawks owner Ben Kerner before a game, eventually retired Loscutoff's number.

"Suffice it to say, everybody had at least one or two strong-armed guys who would go after your star, especially if their star had been hit," Sanders said.

Added Cotton Fitzsimmons, now the Phoenix Suns' vice-president: "You fought till the death back then. The money wasn't that good, and when you got to the playoffs, there was more money, so guys were fighting for survival."

Even fans struck a blow for violence. In Syracuse's State Fair Coliseum in the 50s, when opponents stood out of bounds, a demure-looking woman routinely jabbed them in the leg with a hat pin. Another fan yanked their leg hairs.

In 1959, Syracuse rookie center Connie Dierking was inserted in the game in the first quarter. He quickly body-checked Cincinnati center Wayne Embry into the second row. Embry returned to the court, and Dierking hacked him again. Then again.

In less than 10 minutes of the first quarter, Dierking fouled out, the first player in NBA history to collect six personal fouls prior to the onset of the second quarter.

At least Dierking didn't have to worry about technical fouls.

"We were lucky because we didn't get thrown out of games, even though there were a lot of fights," recalled Atlanta Hawks Coach Lenny Wilkens. "They just broke it up, unless it was getting out of hand."

And it did get out of hand on occasion.

In a 1956 game, Loscutoff tore the shorts from an opponent, who fled the court half-naked.

"Jim was a great guy, but he was just a hatchet man, an enforcer," Fitzsimmons said. "I started coaching in the 70s, and there were enforcers like Maurice Lucas and Paul Silas even then. You always tried to have one of those tough guys."

The NBA began to change in the 1960s, as burliness gave way to sleekness. In the late 70s, NBA officials started re-defining the league's image - using rule changes and marketing schemes to emphasize the sport's graceful athleticism and modern charms.

There are still problems, however. During the 1987-88 season, Detroit's Rick Mahorn body-slammed Michael Jordan as Jordan flew toward the hoop. Then Mahorn tossed Bulls Coach Doug Collins into the scorer's table as if he were a grade-school student. He moved onto a heavyweight bout with Charles Oakley.

But as the NBA took off in the 80s, along with salaries, the city game became the chic game and players flocked to weight machines to build powerful Olympian bodies.

"You have big agile people," Lenny Wilkens said. "And if you let them get out of control, someone could get seriously hurt."

No one has ever created a more powerful body than Malone, which makes his transgressions seemingly more violent. But compared to past enforcers, Malone is positively courtly.

Actually, Malone's emotional duke-outs have created as many notorious headlines as his punch-outs.

The Mailman, for example, created a stir in 1992 when he publicly questioned Magic Johnson's decision to come back with the AIDS virus. In '95 he criticized some of the game's biggest stars for seeking to de-certify the players' union.

He's also blasted Generation X players, and publicly

feuded with Utah owner Larry Miller - a close friend - several times.

And that's just for starters.

"I don't like to use the word 'controversy.' I like to use the word 'adversity.' You learn from adversity by dealing with it," Malone said. "Every time adversity happened to me, I hit it straight on and dealt with it."

In 1990, Malone threatened to boycott the all-star game after being snubbed in fan balloting. He also stopped talking to the press. "It hurt," said Malone, who ended up playing in the game. "Everyone knows I'm the best power forward in the game. It was a slap in the face."

The Mailman went out the next night and poured in 61 points and grabbed 18 rebounds in only 33 minutes during the Jazz' 144-96 win over the Milwaukee Bucks, who'd never experienced a worse defeat.

"I knew Karl wanted to make a statement," then – Bucks coach Del Harris said. "I just didn't know he was going to write a whole book. I told him before the game that if he wanted to make a statement, then he should do it while the issue is hot and not play tonight."

Prior to the start of the 1997-98 season, at the apex of his career, Malone said, "No. 1 on my list of grievances has been disrespect and that feeling won't go away."

In fact, Malone's obsessive need for respect has been an integral part of his game since he entered the NBA.

"I'm Karl and Karl is supposed to work more than the next guy on the team," he said. "Karl is supposed to do a lot of things, and a lot of people don't want to give me credit, and sometimes it (ticks) you off."

Malone went into verbal overdrive in the 1997-98 season. He berated teammate Greg Ostertag for arriving at camp out of shape. He declared he wanted to play with a great center before he retires, which seemingly eliminated the Jazz. He demanded a trade if Coach Jerry Sloan wasn't given a contract extension.

On a national talk show, he expressed a desire to finish his career in "rain country" which seemed to limit his options to Seattle, Portland, Vancouver or perhaps London.

In mid-spring, he said if the Jazz didn't fire KFNZ afternoon radio hosts David Locke and Tom Nissalke, he wanted out. "It's me or them," he said.

Meanwhile, he appeared with Dennis Rodman to promote a tag-team wrestling match, which surprised some since he and The Worm were hardly buddies.

In his book *Bad as I Wanna Be*, Rodman wrote: "There are too many guys in the league like ...Karl Malone, guys who are too high-class to say anything to me. They're too ... white collar to bother with some lowlife bum like me."

Malone and Jazz owner Larry Miller are either friends or enemies, depending on the day.

During Game Five of the 1994 Western Conference playoff series against the Denver Nuggets, Miller left his courtside seat, moved near the team's bench, and screamed at Coach Jerry Sloan to yank Malone.

The outburst flabbergasted Malone and Sloan, although civil wars have become increasingly common.

During a practice for an Orlando-Chicago playoff game, Magic Coach Brian Hill berated Shaq for a blown assignment.

Shaq fired back: "You can't coach anyway. That's the problem. Every time there's a big game, your drawstrings tighten."

Michael Jordan doesn't always keep his wagging tongue in diplomatic place, either. According to *The Jordan Rules*, he has "…been known to lead the team in mooing like a cow when Krause would appear in the locker room (others would hum the theme from *Green Acres*) … Jordan was the one who nicknamed the G.M. 'Crumbs.' " ("He always had doughnut crumbs on his lapels," Jordan says.)

When Krause asked Jordan to call Tony Kukoc to ask him to play for the Bulls, Jordan replied, "I don't speak no Yugoslavian."

But Miller's outburst at Malone was over the top because it was a public matter, much as Latrell Sprewell's assault on Golden State Coach P.J. Carlesimo would later be.

"I know in the past Larry and I have had our disagreements with this contract, but it never came down to this," he said. "So then you sit back and say … 'Is this what he's been wanting to say to me all this time? Is this how he really felt about me? I say no, but damn, why did he get on TV and (have this tirade). I hate having a (bad) game and he was probably having a tough time, and boom, it just happened.'

"It hurt me 50 more times than it (angered) me. It's almost like losing a loved one. You don't know what to do. Every now and then, I can still feel the pain. "

In the tense Jazz locker room afterward, Sloan did his best to smooth things over. In 1990, however, the coach kicked Miller out of the same locker room in a fit of rage.

Generation X players bring out Malone's deepest wrath, including:

• Isiah Rider, who called a press conference to criticize coach Minnesota Timberwolves Coach Bill Blair.

• Chris Webber, who forced the Golden State Warriors to deal him to the Washington Bullets because he didn't care for Don Nelson, one of the game's most respected coaches. Webber was largely responsible for Nelson's departure.

• Norm Van Exel, who shoved referee Ron Garretson into the scorer's table during a game in Denver, then accused Garretson of deliberately jumping into the table to make him look bad.

• Allen Iverson, who was named Player of the Week, after averaging 44.5 points during a four-game stretch, although his team lost all four games.

"It's a mockery of the game," Malone said. 'Oh-and-five and you score 40? So what?' "

• Derrick Coleman, who informed management he had no intention of abiding by the club's just-announced dress code. He wrote a check to account for every ensuing fine.

"There's a new breed of players and it's a new day and

During his rookie year, Karl Malone made only 48% of his free throws, which could've doomed him to a mediocre career. After all, if a power forward is afraid to go to the line, how can he play aggressively? But with a lot of hard work, and plenty of help from Utah coach Frank Layden, the Mailman overcame his foul-shooting problems. *Photo by Steve Lipofsky.*

In the face of tremendous pressure, Utah coach Jerry Sloan has stuck with a time-tested system that has "brought out the best in Malone." The NBA Finals battles between the Jazz and the Bulls have become part of the sport's lore. "They're giving us everything we can ask for," Bulls forward Scottie Pippen said in the 1997 Finals. "It's been very difficult for us. It's more difficult for us than any team we've faced in the finals. *Photo by Steve Lipofsky.*

Utah has mastered the two-man game with John Stockton and Malone. For Stockton, the Mailman is the ultimate target: big, agile, determined. For Malone, Stockton is the ultimate delivery man. This is how Stockton appears to Malone when they connect on the court. *Photo by Steve Lipofsky.*

During his rookie year, Malone couldn't hit the Great Salt Lake with his jumper. But over the years he's developed an array of shots, which have forced defenses to come to the perimeter to defend him. *Photo by Bill Smith.*

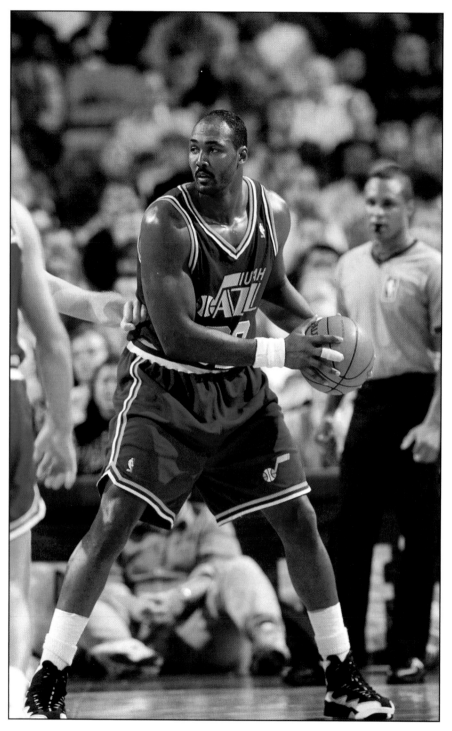

Over the years, Malone has become a shrewd evaluator of defenses. He can hurt opponents in a variety of ways, and he has the patience to wait for his best option. *Photo by Steve Lipofsky.*

Often times, Malone is unstoppable, especially when he's on the scoring end of the fast break. *Photo by Steve Lipofsky.*

Hitting the boards is as natural for Malone as breathing. He's scored more than 25,000 points and pulled down more than 10,000 rebounds in his NBA career, a milestone previously reached only by Wilt Chamberlain, Kareem Abdul-Jabbar, Elvin Hayes and Moses Malone. *Photo by Steve Lipofsky.*

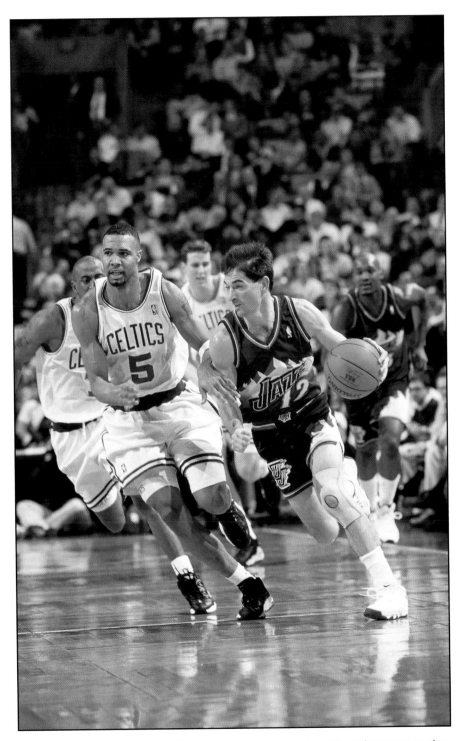

When John Stockton is peeling up court, only good things happen to the Jazz, especially to Malone, who is the ultimate beneficiary of Stockton's handiwork. *Photo by Steve Lipofsky.*

Because of Karl Malone's intimidating size and speed, few defenders are will-ing to block his path to the basket. Taking the charge against the Mailman is akin to willingly standing in front of a speeding bus. *Photo by Steve Lipofsky.*

In October, 1994, the Jazz and Chicago Bulls played an exhibition game in Chicago's new arena, the United Center. It would be the scene of a few more Jazz-Bulls games in the ensuing years. *Photo by Bill Smith.*

The Mailman isn't universally loved by officials, who have called more technical fouls on him than all but a few players. Those players include Dennis Rodman and Charles Barkley. *Photo by Steve Lipofsky.*

By the mid 90s, Malone had become increasingly frustrated by the Jazz' inability to advance to the NBA Finals. "Utah has been known to crumble at the end," San Antonio forward Terry Cummings understated. *Photo by Steve Lipofsky.*

With the addition of Bryon Russell, the Jazz' luck began to change. In the 1996 playoffs, the team made it to the Western Conference Championship, where it lost to Seattle in Game Seven. But Utah would make it to the Finals the next two seasons. *Photo by Steve Lipofsky.*

Malone can "break-down" a defense with his perimeter game, inside game, and, when necessary, he can put the ball onto the floor and shoot off the dribble. *Photo by Bill Smith.*

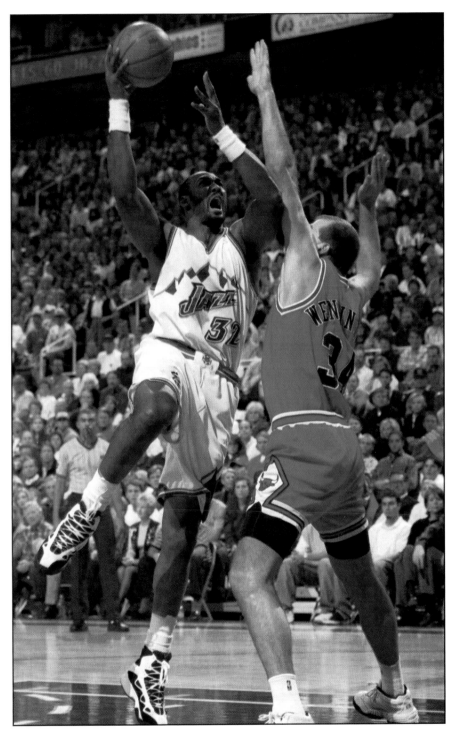

In a preview of the NBA Finals that season, Malone goes up for a basket against the Chicago Bulls' Bill Wennington during a November game in Salt Lake City in 1996. *Photo by Steve Lipofsky.*

Malone is widely regarded as the fastest big man in NBA history. "I've watched a hundred times when he gets a rebound, outlets it to me and then beats me down to the other end of the court to get an open lay-up," John Stockton said. *Photo by Steve Lipofsky.*

The battle between Malone and Dennis Rodman provided an intriguing sub-text to the Bulls-Jazz championship showdowns. "He's just an average player to me," Rodman said. *Photo by Bill Smith.*

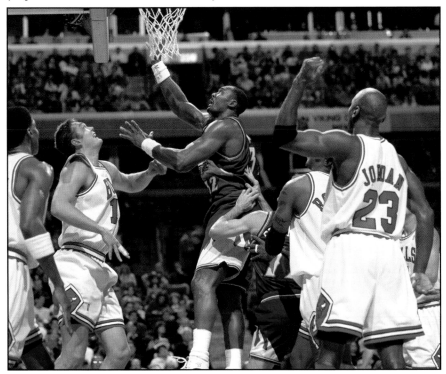

Malone operates on the inside against the Bulls. *Photo by Bill Smith.*

In the history of the NBA, no tandem has ever run the pick and roll to perfection like Karl Malone and John Stockton, who have used the play as the foundation for two title runs vs the Bulls. *Photo by Bill Smith.*

age," Coleman said. "We speak our minds and we have opinions and a lot of people can't deal with that. They can't deal with our names and our status."

Malone is hardly alone in his feelings about Generation X stars.

"I have spent a lifetime in basketball and I am here to tell you that something is terribly wrong," Cleveland Cavs GM Wayne Embry said.

"We have 21-year-old kids making 50 million dollars before they've played their first NBA game. We have players running around with guns and players openly defying their coaches. We can't find enough good young players with basic shooting skills and other fundamentals."

The 1998 All-Star game nearly demoralized Malone. When he arrived at New York's LaGuardia Airport he saw a fleet of limos, none for him. He took a cab to the New York Hilton, but the room was a disaster.

"It was so small I could turn on a TV with my toes," he said.

After being awakened at dawn by the sound of jackhammers, the NBA's reigning MVP phoned the league to find out why he didn't get a limo and fancy digs.

No one does, he was told, which Malone disputed.

"I guess I'm not crazy enough or bad enough or controversial enough to make a fuss over," he said

"This is no longer a basketball game. It's a celebrity tournament and that's not me."

In many ways, Malone has become an iconoclastic

figure in the superstar world within the NBA.

While Jordan and Co. prefer Armani suits, Mercedes sedans and celebrity golf tournaments, Malone sticks to jeans, cowboy boots, trucks and fishing. In fact, some suggest he's a "black redneck," in part because he passionately endorses Salt Lake City.

"He's an Uncle Tom, an Uncle Tom since the beginning of time. He's not real. He's just fake. He talks a good game," Coleman said.

Responded Malone: "If I'm a Uncle Tom and I'm selling out my race, if that's what he means, then I don't know what to say. A lot of the younger players don't know Karl Malone. They only know what some of their buddies say, and they don't know Karl Malone. Do I lose any sleep because younger players don't like me? Hell, no. Do I lose any sleep because older players don't like me? He'll no. You don't have to like me, but you're going to respect me, and that's all that matters."

A *Slam* magazine article added to the controversy in its October 28 issue that many regard Malone as "…the white negro…. The anti-black. The brotha from another planet … Malone on his Harley Davidson, with cowboy boots, with a CAT Diesel (not Shaq diesel) cap on represents something foreign. Something blacks may not be ready for."

In the same article, ESPN analyst David Aldridge said, "Living and playing in Utah, I believe has had an effect on him. By nature everyone is a creature of the circumstances in which they live. Karl is no different. He's just doing what he has to do to survive.

"I don't think Karl Malone has to apologize for anything in his career. What should he have to apologize for. And to whom?"

Malone, characteristically, makes no apologies for his actions or statements.

"I'm not a politician," he told *Sports Illustrated*. "And as far as the black thing goes, well, I'm not oblivious to black causes. But when anyone asks me, I just say, 'Look I'm not your man.' All I know is that the people here accepted me as a person, and I accepted them. The best thing that could've happened to Karl Malone, was coming to Salt Lake City.

"You may not be a better player than me and make more money and all of that, but you aren't going to be any happier than me. I have a life outside of basketball, and I'm comfortable and happy in that life."

"Identity is something we're all in search of," he told *Sport*. "For instance, when Michael (Jordan) started playing golf and got a lot of coverage, everybody wanted to play golf. I've never been like that. I've always been the kind of guy that sort of danced to his own music, meaning (fishing) is what I like.

"I know it's weird, but it's what I want. As athletes, we are big kids. And big kids do get jealous. Some of the things that have been said about me are out of spite, meaning I don't do things that they do. I don't get my notoriety by golfing. I got my notoriety by doing the same things Karl Malone likes to do."

Are celebrity golf tournaments really so important?

"That's what I'm saying," he said.

"I don't get invited to play in charity games and I don't play golf."

In an article in the *Deseret News*, reporter Richard Evans suggested many of Malone's feelings and actions stem from his father's suicide.

"(He's) genuinely quicker than other players to notice when he's booed, when he's slighted by the media, when he feels team management hasn't dealt fairly with him," he wrote.

"While he's become tougher through the years, there's still a vulnerable side to Malone, the little kid who's lost a father and doesn't understand why. In ways too convoluted for most of us to understand, the pursuit for respect has propelled Malone and continue to drive him to prove that he can erase the doubts, even if they're his alone."

In a 1997 *New York Times* article, Malone conceded his father's death still shapes his attitudes.

"It was kind of like hanging over my head, my father not being around, and I was always upset that he wasn't, and that it was his own decision that he wasn't. I didn't accept that.

"It's what drives me now. I'm afraid not to work hard. I'm afraid not to work out in the summer. I'm afraid to fail. I still haven't said, 'I've made it.'

"I could never be the kid I wanted to be."

Chapter Six

Still Trucking After All These Years

Twenty-five years ago, as Karl Malone's hunger for glory began to stretch beyond Summerville's confining borders, the future of the best basketball player in rural Louisiana suddenly fell into place.

Malone had the size, ambition and big-fisted dexterity to go all the way in his chosen field, and he knew it, as did Shirley Turner, who was the first to hear of his big plans.

"Mama," Malone said, "Some day I'm gonna own me a big truck.'"

Guess what?

In 1992, Malone started Malone Enterprises, which delivers potatoes, lumber and other goods to states in the West. Within a year, he had six drivers and seven trucks, as well as his own personal 57-foot rig which featured a

Western mural on one side, and a mural of himself in cowboy gear in another.

Malone once drove a load from Idaho to Utah and back. At every stop, he was asked for his autograph.

"I'm not your average deliveryman," concedes the Mailman.

Malone is not your average guy. In fact, he's an interesting bunch of guys: pitchman, rancher, businessman, auto dealer, hunter, fisherman, wrestler, actor, husband, father.

He doesn't live in your average house(s) either.

The Mailman owns a $5 million, 27,000-square-foot dream home on two acres of prime Utah real estate that features a pool with a waterslide, a waterfall in the foyer and logs shipped in from Oregon that create a rustic look.

He owns a cattle ranch in El Dorado, Ark., a fishing cabin on the Kenai River in Alaska and a snowmobile lodge in Idaho.

The Mailman also owns plenty of motorcycles, cars and other high-tech toys, not to mention several businesses.

But those are only trappings.

In Karl's world, everything turns around one dream. And it's not basketball. It's trucking. Nothing takes a back seat to that.

"Basketball is my job, but this is my love," he said. "It's the whole thing: the machinery, the companionship with the other drivers, the smell of the diesel.

"I'm a careful driver - when you've got a 10,000-pound

tractor, a 10,000-pound trailer and a 60,000-pound payload in the back, you've got to be - but I'd be lying if I said I didn't like the feeling of being the most powerful thing on the road, yet under control, too. You know what I feel like when I'm driving. A runaway truck under control."

When he was 20, a Louisiana Tech alum who owned a trucking company let the Mailman make his rookie run in an 18-wheeler. He was euphoric.

At that point, Malone began the long haul to become a fully accredited driver. He talked to other drivers, studied mechanics, worked on driving skills and ultimately, in 1992, passed the exam on his first nervous try.

As part of the test, Malone had to parallel park a 48-foot truck in a 58-foot space.

"I wish I could describe that feeling of satisfaction," he told *Sports Illustrated*. "On my way home after passing, I climbed in the truck, rolled up the windows and yelled for 10 minutes straight. I was trying to keep cool when I came home, but Kay took one look at me and said, 'You got it right?' Hey, you just can't be cool about some things."

Lynn Thompson, who administered the test, said: "Karl went through every single step we'd put any potential driver through. Being a professional athlete, sure, his reflexes and strength help him as a driver. But his intelligence is just as important. He's going to represent the industry well."

Malone paid nearly $200,000 for his custom-made and custom-painted fleet leader and ordered six more trucks at an estimated cost of $115,000 each shortly afterward.

Malone was so proud of his first rig he drove it to practice to show it off to teammates.

"When people saw the first truck," he said. "they looked at me like I was crazy. They said, 'What are you doing?' But it's a promotional truck, too. Besides, it's the one I drive. I wanted to make a statement with it.

"Not only is the truck company closest to my heart, it's by far the biggest investment I've made.

"I'm not out to steal anybody's business. But I know what we can do. I know what service we can provide. If people are looking for a neat, clean dependable truck that can get products from point A to B on time, they need to see me.

"A lot of guys have dreams about what they want to do when they retire," he told *Sports Illustrated.* "But I'm already living my dreams.

Malone realized another boyhood dream when he acquired a 190-acre cattle ranch and haycutting operation near El Dorado, Ark.

"I get up in the morning, sit on the porch, have a cup of coffee and watch those cows grazing out there in the field."

In the early 90s, Malone opened a retail apparel business in a Salt Lake City shopping mall.

He also became pitchman for several national products, including Rogaine and LA Gear.

"I'd go crazy if I only had basketball," he said. "You can't even imagine the respect I have for the NBA. I do have a life, though. I have a wife and two beautiful kids. I've been blessed enough to have a couple companies that are going pretty well."

The Jazz wasn't worried about Malone's expanding business empire. His play continued to improve each year and his training regimen was second to none.

But Frank Layden realized the potential problems in having a superstar with too many interests. In San Antonio, Spurs Coach Larry Brown was repeatedly frustrated by David Robinson's inability to focus solely on basketball.

"I get a lot of enjoyment out of a lot of different things," Robinson said in *The Force.* "Music, people, basketball. But if I'm thinking about my girl, or music, in a game, I drift. If I come into a game focused, I stay focused. Magic (Johnson) was focused for years because basketball was his main interest.

"I came in this league with other interests and had to learn to sacrifice things for basketball. Life's a learning process. I have to learn to sacrifice things for basketball, but I can't lose my identity. What good is it being the greatest basketball player if you're the most miserable?"

Spurs Coach Gregg Popovich, then an assistant, learned quickly that Robinson's mind could be in several places at once.

"The game's not in his blood. One day I showed him something in practice. He said, 'I almost got it. A couple more months should do it.' He meant a concerto he was composing on his keyboard."

Added Robinson: "Sometimes I just find myself watching, kind of spacing out, not forcing myself to go down and get into action."

Even Michael Jordan downloads at times.

"Sometimes I'll just sit in a chair and look out a window and try to clear my mind," he said. "I find it peaceful, and I wish I could do it more. But then something always comes up."

Often it's a business matter.

In fact, Jordan's business pursuits are as remarkable as his on-court achievements. His Nike 'Air Jordans' made $130 million the first year. With the help of Spike Lee's Mars Blackmon commercials, sales soon rose to $200 million.

By 1992, agent David Falk's shrewd deals were earning him $20 million a year, making Jordan the first black commercial superstar.

"(Jordan) has a level of value as a commercial spokesman that is almost beyond comprehension," a prominent ad executive said in *The Golden Boys.* "It never happened before and may not happen ever again."

Yet Jordan never loses his focus on the court. Neither does Malone, although his commercial endeavors are minuscule compared to Jordan's.

After shooting 16-of-42 against Chicago in the first two games of the 1997 NBA Finals, he was wounded to the point of humiliation. Before Game Three, he hopped onto his Harley for a 40-minute ride through the canyon land near Salt Lake City and ultimately to the Delta Center.

"Even though I was coming to the game, I didn't feel like I was. I kind of felt I was there somewhere else," he said after leading the Jazz to a 104-93 win.

"What I was thinking while I was riding my Harley was: 'Just block everything out.' "

Malone goes his own way in the off-season as well.

"I love things athletes aren't supposed to like," he told *The Sporting News*. "I guess I like cowboy boots, I love my four-wheel drive trucks, I love getting back on my ranch back home. I love driving the (18-wheel) tractor. I love to hunt and to fish. That's what I mean by free spirit.

"That's why I'd see myself coming back as a bald eagle if I came back an animal, something that's not confined. When I'm playing basketball, I'm like that."

Actually, the NBA hierarchy has embraced Malone because he appeals to most demographic groups, especially women, a growing force in the league.

For years, only hard-core female fans attended NBA games. But in the early 80s, women broke through the barriers into arenas, and wave after wave have followed, fueled by a massive NBA marketing effort to make them and their families feel at home.

By the time the 90s are over, women could make it the She Decade in the NBA.

League officials estimate up to 40% of fans at a typical game are women. And the number is rising.

"We've always had more women fans than other sports," NBA vice-president Paula Hanson said. "But we make a real effort to reach out to women and families. We try to sell ourselves as an entertainment option, not just a sports option."

In the 80s and 90s, women understand the nuances of basketball because they've played it. That makes it much easier for the NBA, especially compared with football and baseball.

"I'd say nine out of ten have played the sport at some point of their lives, either shooting around with their sons or daughters out in front or in gym class," said Terry Lyons, an NBA executive. "There are very few high school girls who are graduating these days who have not seen or played basketball."

Malone's personality is part of his game. You can practically hear the gears working in his head. You can see his emotions on his face.

What do you see at an NFL game? A helmet head, pounds of padding and an actual face every now and then - in the distance below. And baseball? Uniforms, hats, home plate, big walls.

"A lot of the interest from women is due to the fact the players are very identifiable," Hanson said. "It's easier to get to know them, and you can see the emotions of the game.

For several years, Malone was one of the NBA's most sought-after bachelors, rivaling Charles Barkley, his friend, who described in *Outrageous!* about what it's like to be a target of mass female desire.

"I've received boxes filled with roses, candy, cookies, cake and even underwear. On the road, such deliveries are regular occurrences, like mints on my pillow. It's a scream. Dominos Delivers Desire."

In the ABA, Wendell Ladner was as famous for his love of women as his love of the game.

"His vocabulary was pretty much limited to basketball and women," Denver Nuggets general manager Dan Issel said. "And he talked a lot more about women than basketball."

The Kentucky Colonels had Ladner pose for a "hairy-chested" poster that was meant to imitate Burt Reynolds famous pose in *Cosmopolitan* magazine. The posters sold out within a day.

Sex and the NBA have always been intertwined. Wilt Chamberlain claimed in a book he'd slept with more than 20,000 women during and after his NBA career.

In Chicago, a woman threw herself on the ground in front of Michael Jordan's car while he was leaving Chicago Stadium. At one point, Jordan dated Robin Givens, who eventually married Mike Tyson. That was a sobering moment for Jordan, who realized he'd been little more than a commodity.

"It was hard for me to trust a woman's alleged affections because it was difficult for me to know whether she liked me for what I had or who I was.

"I realized it was hard for many people meeting me to separate me the successful player from me that man."

The party life has seduced many would-be Hall-of-Famers into a career-killing lifestyle.

Gene Littles, formerly head coach of the Charlotte Hornets, recalled in *Loose Balls* how Marvin Barnes self-destructed with the Spirits of St. Louis.

"The Spirits were a bunch of young guys let loose in the city who had money for the first time in their lives. They didn't think about anything but what made them happy right now. It was all big cars, fancy clothes and fast women. One time Marvin was late for a practice in training camp. (Coach) Bob MacKinnon asked him why he was late and Marvin said, 'I lost my car in a lot downtown.' "

"MacKinnon said, 'What kind of car is it?' "

Marvin said, "A Bentley."

There couldn't have been three Bentleys in all of St. Louis. A blind man could pick out a Bentley in a parking lot. Just looking at MacKinnon, you could see that Fly (Williams) and Marvin aged him at least 10 years that season."

Malone met his wife inadvertently, and quickly settled into a quiet life.

In 1988, Kay Kinsey, visiting her sister in Salt Lake City, saw the Mailman signing autographs at the Fashion Place Mall.

"Who's that?" she asked.

"The Mailman," answered her brother-in-law.

"You mean the first black postmaster of Utah is signing autographs?" Kinsey asked.

"(He's) one of the best basketball players in the NBA," she was informed.

Kinsey, the just-retired Miss Idaho, approached Malone for an autograph.

"When I walked up to Karl, he handed me that old line - 'Is this for your husband? Your boyfriend?' I said, 'No, I don't have one.' My sister took our picture. Karl said when it developed I could mail it to him and he would sign it for me. I kind of rolled my eyes and said, 'Thanks.' "

Months later, Kinsey sent the picture. It didn't take long for the Mailman to call.

"This is Karl Malone."

She hung up.

Malone called back.

"No I promise. This is Karl Malone. You wrote me a letter and sent this picture of you as Miss Idaho."

In any city, the celebrity life is usually two-thirds burden and one-thirds blessing.

In Dallas, for example, Cowboys quarterback Troy Aikman buys groceries by E-mail, shops at department stores after hours, and, for casual conversation, checks into computer chat rooms - under a fake name.

He's been stalked by several women, one of whom accused him of turning her into a prostitute, another who ended up in jail and two who swam in his pool late at night after sneaking onto his property.

In Denver, John Elway's life can be a trial as well. In 1989, he went national with his complaints about Denver.

"(The media) talk about my hair, they talk about my teeth, they talk about how much I tip, how much I drink, how I'm playing ...I'm sick of it. I'm about to suffocate.

"I don't want to sound like a crybaby, so I don't talk about it. But it's just gotten to be too much lately. I'm just torn up inside."

Elway's wife, Janet, has been stunned by the hostility level of her husband's critics, especially during the 1980s, before John began to silence all critics.

"When we got married, I knew he'd be a public figure, but I had no idea. When I would go into a department store or grocery store and sign a check, they would say, well, no good things about John."

When Elway threw five interceptions against Kansas City, Janet thought about fleeing Mile High Stadium for ...anywhere.

"There was this guy sitting behind me who just wouldn't let up," she said. "Finally, he yelled, 'Hey Elway, you can get your g.d. wife pregnant but you can't complete a so-and-so pass.' I turned around slapped him across the face. He was pretty shocked and I wasn't very proud of myself for doing it.

"They forget the players and their families are real people, too."

But Michael Jordan lives on a planet of his own. In fact, when people actually see him, not his ubiquitous image, their reactions are almost eerie.

In *Hang Time, Chicago Tribune* columnist Bob Greene, described the phenomenon: "When the game ended and the Bulls were leaving the floor on their way to the stairs that led down to the locker room, I saw for the first time what I would later see every time I was in Jordan's company.

"Several hundred people had gathered just to look at him. They were being held back by ushers and security guards, and they weren't yelling. They were just staring. As he walked quickly by with the rest of the Bulls, all of those eyes bored right into him. Every set of silent eyes. It gave me chills. It was almost creepy."

For Jordan, it was just a fact of life.

"You can feel the eyes," he said. "I don't want to make too much of a point of it, but it's like the eyes are burning into you. It never goes away, not even for one second."

For much of his career, Malone led a charmed life in Salt Lake City, where civility is a prized virtue.

On the other hand, there are no other major-league franchises, so privacy is a rare commodity.

"It's like a college atmosphere," Jazz guard Jeff Malone said.

Even marginal players are celebrities.

Mark Eaton, who played for the Jazz in the 80s, remembers watching people drive by his home, stop and videotape it. Jazz forward Larry Krystkowiak added that fans used to knock on his apartment door and ask for autographs.

"The lifestyle can be lonely," Kay Malone told the *Salt Lake Tribune*. "We can't go to movies or out to dinner because people ask for autographs. Women are always waiting for him after games, leaving him messages. I've received obscene phone calls, and women make rude remarks to me. You learn who your friends are. There are moments when I wish I was a schoolteacher and Karl was a construction worker and we could sit in front of the television and say, 'Wow. There's Michael Jordan!'

"Strangers come up and say, 'Tell your husband to quit talking and just shoot the ball or they ask me if he is on the court. When I hear those things, I can only imagine what they say to Karl. It makes me want to go home and just hold him and tell him how sorry I am. But he's such a strong person. Nothing breaks him down.' "

Nevertheless, after the 1998 season, Malone was caught off guard when many Utahans criticized his decision to start a pro wrestling career. That angered him, as did the Jazz' management's decision to send him a letter, reportedly warning that a wrestling injury could void his contract.

During an ESPN interview, Malone didn't rule out playing for another team after his contract expires in the summer of 1999.

"Everything I do or say, I'm headlines in Utah," he said. "If Karl Malone is in L.A. or New York, it would be no big deal. A lot of things (in the summer of 1998) have been said and done that could affect on me staying in Utah. There's a time in your life when you have to look at every option. You have to allow yourself to be a little selfish."

Malone has done his share of good works. He bought

a fence for his former elementary school to keep children from wandering onto a nearby highway. He gave money and guidance to a Brooklyn teenager whose family lived in a shelter for the homeless.

He rapped Charles Barkley on the knuckles for his "I'm not a role model" spiel.

"Charles, you can deny being a role medal all you want, but I don't think it's your decision to make," he wrote in an article for *Sports Illustrated*. "We don't choose to be role models, we are chosen. Our only choice is whether to be a good role model or a bad one."

Malone also established the Karl Malone Foundation for Kids in 1997 and is involved in the local Prevention of Child Abuse and Children's Justice Center.

"I love kids," he said. "If I can have 10, I will."

In fact Malone said he and his wife have considered adopting twin boys.

"I just love the sounds of kids," he said.

But in a copyrighted story in July, 1998, the *Salt Lake Tribune* reported that in his hometown of Summerville, La., three children, 17-year-old twins Daryl and Cheryl Ford, as well as 14-year-old Demetrius Bell, all believe Malone is their father. Paternity suits against Malone were all settled out of court.

In June, 1998, he met with the Ford twins, born the summer after Malone graduated from high school. Bell, however, was not invited to the reunion, which only increased his pain.

Gloria Bell was only 13 when she gave birth to

Demetrius during Malone's sophomore season at Louisiana Tech. Demetrius is much like the man he claims is his father: he's a big fan of trucks and likes to hunt and fish. But he prefers softball to basketball for a simple reason.

"Demetrius is ashamed that his dad doesn't claim him," Bell told the *Salt Lake Tribune.* "I've told him that's not his fault. But he shies away from anything that has to do with Karl. It hurts his feelings when he goes somewhere and everybody's talking about Karl Malone."

Bell wasn't alone in her feelings.

"He just never did accept them," added Postmistress Edna Brown. "It's caused a lot of hard feelings."

The Ford twins both play high school basketball. Cheryl wears No. 32 - the same as Malone - and played on a Junior Olympic team that visited Moscow recently. Daryl, a 198-pound forward, was a star on the local high school team.

Malone's actions contradicted his well-known views on parenting and Cheryl says her father contacted her only after a supermarket tabloid broke the story.

Cheryl clearly resembles Karl. In fact, she says strangers often approach her in malls to ask if she's related.

"I didn't have to tell them," she said. "They could look at me and tell."

Some in Summerfield believe that if Malone is the father, it obviously contradicts his statements about never forgetting his roots.

"Everybody around her is proud of Karl, of what he has done" a woman told the *Salt Lake Tribune*. "But then you see these kids day in and day out. I can't imagine the pain they have had to grow up with."

Frank Layden, a surrogate father to Malone, came to his defense in his hour of personal crises.

"It seems to be an unfortunate incident he's trying to correct," Layden told the *Tribune*.

"But personally I'm not going to love Karl Malone any less. Because of all he's done and all he's accomplished, he has cemented this community like no other person in history with the possible exception of Brigham Young. He's done many nice things for so many people. I'd go so far as to say he's one of the most generous, giving people I know. He's generous and giving almost to a fault."

Added Layden: "When people start casting stones at Karl Malone, they'd better live in a brick house."

Chapter Seven

All That Jazz

The Utah Jazz has been dealing itself into NBA lore for years, but it nearly became history before producing it.

In 1979, few believed the Jazz would even survive in Utah or anywhere else for that matter; not after five years in the Big Easy, which was inaptly named for Sam Battistone's start-up franchise.

To critics, Salt Lake City was worse than New Orleans; it was a suburb to I-70 and little more.

"I didn't think the community was big enough or that the building was adequate and that we'd be gone in three years to Anaheim," Frank Layden said. "I mean the ABA Utah Stars won a title and folded two years later. I really thought it was a stopover."

Layden stayed over in Salt Lake City, along with son Scott, John Stockton, Karl Malone, Larry Miller, Jerry Sloan and the rest of the cast of characters who eventually transformed the modern Jazz into one of America's most intriguing sports stories.

Pete Maravich, meanwhile, is the symbol of the bad old days, when the Jazz was a burlesque of a basketball team.

And that's a minor tragedy.

Maravich was the most creative offensive talent in the history of the game, a pathfinder who made circus shots and between-the-legs dribbling an acceptable part of the game at every level.

But he got lost in limbo in the NBA, especially with the Jazz, whose ineptness from the top down sheathed his brilliance.

At LSU, Pistol Pete averaged 43.8, 44.2 and 44.5 ppg in three seasons, and set NCAA records for points in a season (1,381) and career (3,667), as well as the highest career scoring average (44.2).

During a game against St. John's, Maravich made a 40-footer at the buzzer for his 39th and 40th points - of the second half. The St. John's team rushed onto the court to embrace the sophomore, already a folk hero.

"He was an American phenomenon, a stepchild of the human imagination," ex-Jazz teammate Rich Kelley said.

As his legend grew, Pistol Pete made a movie of his tricky moves and circus shots. A coach of an all-black high school team in Baton Rouge went slack-jawed when he saw it.

"My God, he's one of us," he said.

Maravich was the third pick in the 1970 draft and signed a $1.5 million five-year deal with the Atlanta Hawks. Fans streamed in from throughout the South to see his show, but the Hawks pressured him to play a team game. The losses started piling up.

Maravich hoped for a reprieve when he was traded to the expansion New Orleans Jazz in 1974.

But the Jazz lost 13 of its first 14 games, which cost coach Scotty Robertson his job. He was replaced by Butch van Breda Kolff, who didn't do much better until the stretch run, when the Jazz won 18 of its final 35 games.

In 1975-76 the Jazz won 15 more games than in their first year, finishing with a 38-44 record. In 1976-77 Elgin Baylor replaced van Breda Kolff and the Jazz compiled a 35-47 record.

Meanwhile, Maravich averaged 31.1 points per game, best in the league, and often played brilliantly.

Something was missing, however. Pistol Pete's genius stems from the impulsiveness that most coaches abhorred. At LSU, he played for his father, Press, who never restricted his repertoire of silky moves. But he never enjoyed that freedom in the NBA, which blunted his magic.

Nonetheless, he'd advanced much further than most playground geniuses, including Earl "The Goat" Manigault, whose stunts on New York City's playgrounds were legendary: leaping to place a quarter on the top of the backboard or reverse dunking a basketball 36 straight times to win a $60 bet.

"Occasionally, he would drive past a few defenders, dunk the ball with one hand, catch it with the other - and raise it and stuff it through a hoop a second time before returning to earth," author Pete Axthelm wrote in *The City Game.*

But Manigault couldn't deal with constraints of organized ball.

In 1971, he received a tryout with the ABA's Utah Stars, but the incredible leaper who made dunking an art form couldn't even make the squad. He died of heart failure at 53 in 1998 after a long battle against heroin abuse.

Even at his worst, Maravich was sublime.

When Los Angeles Laker Marv Roberts moved from the ABA to the NBA, and watched Pistol Pete for the first time, he jumped off the Lakers bench and began pointing and shouting. "I sees ya, Pete, I sees ya."

But the pressure to win a championship was unraveling Maravich, who became increasingly paranoid as fans, he perceived, turned on him.

"We get beat by 43 and I get blamed," he told *Sports Illustrated's* Curry Kirkpatrick.

"LSU was Tigertown and lots of laughs," Ronnie, his brother said. "Then suddenly there was no Tigertown. Pete wasn't a hero anymore. When people got on him ...he's been shell-shocked ever since."

On Feb. 20, 1977 Pistol Pete began sinking rainbow jumpers and twisting runners and fadeaways against the New York Knicks, and didn't stop until game's end. It was like the old days in Tigertown, as Maravich finished with 68 points and head-shaking praise from those who watched this rare display of brilliance.

"But as morning rolled around the next day," he wrote in his autobiography, "I wanted nothing more than to stay in bed and hope the world would somehow disappear. All I could think of were the expectations of the New Orleans fans, the club owners, the coach, the players, my dad, and worst of all, myself."

Eleven months after that performance, Maravich injured his knee while attempting a between-the-legs pass, all but ending his career.

He accompanied the Jazz to Salt Lake City and hung around until 1980, when Layden finally released him. Maravich moved on to the Boston Celtics for one last desperate fling, then quit, disgusted with the game.

For three years, Maravich didn't pick up a ball, retreating instead into survivalism and his own darkening paranoia. At one point, he painted a bulls-eye on his roof for - who knows what?

In 1984, while living in self-imposed exile in New Orleans, Maravich finally found peace in his Christian faith and family.

"I know what (success) can do," he told *Sports Illustrated*. "Success buys more liquor, more drugs, more ladies. By being successful, we can destroy ourselves."

"He was probably the most unusual team athlete of his time; certainly he was one of the most misunderstood," Curry Kirkpatrick wrote in a *Sports Illustrated* obituary. "He was Cousy long after Cousy and Magic even before Magic. An entertainer. The one-and-only. The star. As a Louisiana State senior he wrote an *SI* cover story headlined: *I Want to Put on a Show.*

"But it was Pete's terrible misfortune always to be misplaced: He was an individualist in a team game, the white boy in the black man's game, the people's choice who in his increasing paranoia felt the people were against him."

Maravich died of heart disease in 1988 at 40, while playing a game of pick-up basketball in Pasadena. His final words: "I'm really feeling good."

Hot Rod Hundley is also an emblem of those hazy crazy days of the New Orleans Jazz. He was the team's play-by-play announcer, a job he holds today.

Few men were better suited for New Orleans, and less suited for Salt Lake City.

"It's a helluva transition from the French Quarter to the Mormon Tabernacle," he said.

Hundley, whose father was a pool shark and his mother reportedly a madam at a brothel, was a legendary party animal at West Virginia and in the NBA.

He also was a marvelous stylist who set the stage for Maravich.

"Because my parents were divorced and left West Virginia when I was very young, I grew up in a lot of different places with a lot of different people," he said in *Tall Tales*. "I found a home on the playground and stayed there day and night."

During an NIT game at Madison Square Garden, the West Virginia whiz made two free throws – one a left-handed hook, the other a right-handed hook.

"One time I tried a few ball-handling things and fans ate it up," he said in *Tall Tales*. "So once in a while, I'd be at the foul line, and I'd spin the ball on my finger and then shoot by punching the ball. Or I'd shot a free throw with my back to the basket, straight over my head. I made a 20-foot shot from my knees and I threw the ball in from 20 feet - behind my back, and it was a bank shot."

Hundley lasted six seasons with the Lakers, and played on two All-Star teams. But he's remembered as an entertainer first, and player second.

"I look at my NBA career and I realize that I lost my outside shot and my confidence in it," he said. "I don't know why. I do know there are some things I should have done differently. But I don't dwell on that.

"What the hell, I went into the NBA making $10,000 and came out making $11,000, and in between I made two All-Star teams. I was like a guy who goes into the army as a buck private and six years later he comes out still a buck private, but he's got some great stories to tell."

Despite his lifestyle differences, Hundley quickly became a favorite of fans in Salt Lake City. His fast-paced delivery, which has been compared to that of a West Virginia auctioneer, and endless anecdotes enliven even the most boring games.

More importantly, fans trust him.

"His influence is such that if the inflection of his voice suggests that a certain player isn't playing well or shouldn't be in the game, that player will be subjected to being booed," a Jazz insider told *Sports Illustrated*.

For years, Hundley had plenty to criticize.

In 1979, for example, the club traded Leonard "Truck" Robinson to Phoenix for guard Ron Lee, forward Marty Byrnes, two first-round picks and cash. The Jazz responded with an NBA-worst 26-56 record under Baylor.

At that point, with the hangman closing in, Battistone and co-owner Larry Hatfield announced the move to Utah. Frank Layden was hired to be general manager a month later.

Basketball enjoys a special status in Utah. The University of Utah, runner-up in the 1998 Final Four, and Brigham Young have tradition-rich programs. And the Utah Stars won the 1971 ABA title before their demise.

But when Battistone sponsored a contest to select a more appropriate nickname for Salt Lake City's new team, only 100 bothered to reply.

So the New Orleans Jazz officially became the Utah Jazz, which Layden was hard-pressed to explain.

"Yeah, we don't have clubs or bars like New York," he said. "But there is an appreciation for jazz music here."

Layden replaced coach Elgin Baylor with Tom Nissalke, then traded for Adrian Dantley as the 1979-80 season approached. The Jazz finished with a 24-58 record, which at least allowed Layden to select the college player of the year, Louisville guard Darrell Griffith, in the 1980 draft.

But the Jazz plunged to a 28-54 record. After a pitiful

start in 1981, Layden made his shrewdest move yet: he named himself coach.

Meanwhile, financial problems continued to short-circuit Layden's plans. In 1982, the Jazz nearly merged with the Denver Nuggets. In 1983 Battistone announced the club would play as many as 11 home games in Las Vegas.

By scheduling games in Vegas, he hoped to generate extra-revenue and open up a secondary TV market, as well as help a friend help fill some dates at the newly constructed Thomas Mack Center.

The idea didn't exactly take the gambling mecca by storm.

"Hasn't been much in the newspapers about it," Tom Wiesner, a former Las Vegas County Commissioner said following the announcement.

The NBA Board of Governors OK'd the plan, but recommended a ban on betting on all 82 Jazz games.

That outraged sports' book operators, who managed to limit the prohibition to only the games in Las Vegas. Even then, they weren't pleased.

"There are more illegal bookies in New York's Madison Square Garden than in the whole state of Nevada," Las Vegas gambler Lem Baker said. "This is a league full of guys renegotiating contracts and sniffing coke, but they say they're worried about the credibility. If it wasn't for gambling, the NBA wouldn't have made it."

Jazz vice-president David Checketts said the club had no choice but to enact the plan.

"It was the league's concern that anyone coming to these games should cheer just about what's happening out on the floor," he said. "The league doesn't want a situation where Darrell Griffith hits a three-point shot at the buzzer to win a game for the Jazz and people boo him because they have money on another team."

The verbal jostling ended, and the hoopla began, when the Jazz met the Chicago Bulls in its Vegas premier.

It drew 13,186 – the most ever for a Jazz "home" game and for an indoor event in Las Vegas. But it was an odd night. UNLV alums Reggie Theus and Sidney Green played for the Bulls, not the home-away-from-home Jazz, which lost 128-117.

"The Bulls would have beaten us in Chicago or at Niagara Falls," Frank Layden said.

The Jazz and Las Vegas ended the ill-fated experiment the following season.

Beginning in 1983, Layden drafted Thurl Bailey, Stockton and Malone in successive years, establishing the foundation for the modern Jazz.

At the start of the 1983-84 season, Layden told his traveling secretary to book an extended stay in April in San Diego, where the team ended the regular season.

But by the time the San Diego trip rolled around, the Jazz was Midwest Division champions and Layden was busy preparing for a playoff series against Denver as well as acceptance speeches for his Coach and General Manager of the Year awards.

"I constantly lived thinking I was on top of a bubble

that was going to burst," said Layden, whose team had lost 52 games the year before.

To set the tone for the best-of-five series against the Nuggets, the Jazz prepared for a dramatic fireworks display at the Salt Palace.

It blew up in their faces, scattering debris all over the floor, which delayed the start of Game One.

Layden, whose team eventually lost the series in five games, reacted characteristically:

He laughed.

Why not? The Jazz had survived its worst days.

But even in 1997, with the Jazz riding high, Derek Harper refused a trade to Utah, preferring instead to remain with the pitiful Dallas Mavericks.

"They're going to have a hard time getting people to come here to play after John and myself and Jeff Hornacek and Antoine Carr are gone," Malone said. "You have to be a little different to play here. It's really tough for a free agent to come here. This place is not for everybody.

"When I first got here, I looked around and wondered what in the hell have I got myself into? The perception ...about Utah is hard to overcome. I like it here. My wife and I are building our dream home here. Everybody talks about the Mormons. We're Baptist and we don't have any problems."

Larry Miller, a local boy made good, started making all the right moves when he bought a 50% interest in the club in 1985. Two years later, after purchasing the remaining 50%, he saved the franchise from moving to Minnesota. Later he built the Delta Center with the money he earned from his chain of auto dealerships.

In many ways, Miller is the perfect owner: shrewd, patient, resourceful, and driven by a desire to win an NBA title for his native state.

Miller couldn't conceal his emotions from the public because he was so publicly involved.

In 1997, he choked back tears when Karl Malone was awarded the MVP award; yet he screamed wildly at Coach Jerry Sloan to yank the Mailman in Game Five of the 1994 Western Conference semi-finals against Denver.

In that same game, Miller jostled with a Nuggets fan and then banned himself for the next two games to prevent more self-inflicted wounds.

For years, before the opening tip, Miller told refs: "Remember, it's only a game." Then he'd scream and berate them the next couple hours.

"I realized that was inconsistent," he said. "In many ways, my perspective has changed through the years. I'm more clearly defined as to what the Jazz are all about.

"I'm able for the most part to keep a rein on my emotions until I know (the outcome of a game)."

Even now, Miller won't even watch Jazz road games on TV because it invariably unnerves him.

"I have a real hard time dealing with the opposing crowd's energy against us," he said.

Those are traits that endear Miller to many Jazz fans. So does the fact he's an active Mormon.

In fact, Miller has created a special bond between the team and city, as well as among his employees, who are uncommonly loyal.

"Even the secretaries stay," Layden said. "The ushers are 108-years-old, for Pete's sake. No one ever leaves."

In 1998, Malone and Stockton discovered that a Delta Center security guard was quitting because of family concerns. When the guard got home after his final shift, he discovered phone messages from both Malone and Stockton, offering assistance.

"In a lot of other cities, they'd have fired the coach three times by now. They'd have packaged Karl or John and made a change. Not here. Fans are more supportive, and because of that, they've been able to have a successful team for a long period of time," ex-Jazz forward Tom Chambers said.

But the Jazz had little to show for its long run of playoff appearances.

By 1997, it'd been eliminated twice each by Seattle, Portland, Golden State and Houston, once each by Dallas, Phoenix, and the Lakers - and by plodding journeymen like Manute Bol, Mark Aguirre, Kevin Duckworth Frank and Brickowski.

And seven times the end came at home.

In Salt Lake City, hardened critics showed little mercy on talk shows. Of course, a hardened critic in Salt Lake City is indistinguishable from a gentleman caller elsewhere.

"I sure hope they work hard to get over the hump," a

typically irate caller sounded.

Most fans weren't so extreme.

"The people here love the Jazz," Fred Ball, the president of the Salt Lake Area Chamber of Commerce, told *The Sporting News* in 1994. "We're never going to be an NFL city. We're never going to have Major League Baseball. If we're to be major league in anything, it's basketball. And the Jazz is our team. People would go absolutely crazy if the Jazz ever happened to go all the way. But they appreciate the level of play they see now."

In fact, Frank Layden says the Jazz would rather lose with dignity than win with Dennis Rodman.

"We haven't paid the devil to get to the next level," Layden said.

Malone is just as emphatic.

"Is it worth dealing with a coach that I can't sit down with and have dinner with or I can't walk to the back of the plane and sit down and talk about personal stuff? A championship is not worth that to Karl Malone," he said.

Added owner Larry Miller: "If what it took to win a championship was to win 60 games, but have guys I wouldn't want to talk to in the locker room, I wouldn't be in this."

The predominance of the Mormon faith in the state helps explain why Utahans are less demanding than fans of other NBA teams.

"Traditionally, we try to be nice," Robert Kirby, a religion humorist for the *Salt Lake Tribune* told ESPN. "There's something about us. If you're not nice, you go to hell and nobody wants to go to hell, so let's behave ourselves. I guess most Mormons don't want to turn themselves into monsters over something like sports."

Added Malone: "They're very, very forgiving people. Everybody likes to take shots at the Mormons, but they are some of the most forgiving people that I have ever met."

But Miller knows Jazz fans are ultimately like fans everywhere, which means they're inherently impatient.

"I look at our flag and all the things you see around the town, the flag and banners and it's very emotionally gratifying to see that," he said. "I think the Jazz fill a very special role in our community. But at some point we'll probably find out if they come just to watch us because we fit into the culture and they really love the team. Or if they come just to watch us win.

"I hope we don't go through the drought that the Boston Celtics have gone through, but to think we're still going to be championship contenders in the wake of Karl Malone and John Stockton would be foolish."

Perhaps Miller offered an explanation for his reluctance to tinker with his key players - Malone and Stockton and Coach Jerry Sloan – when he commented on rumors that the Chicago Bulls would intentionally disband after the 1998 playoffs.

"I'm very reluctant to try to second-guess (Bulls owner) Jerry Reinsdorf and (General Manager) Jerry Krause, but nevertheless, it is bizarre what might happen.

"The Bulls are a true dynasty. To me, if I'm the guy

making that decision, if I can keep the thing economically viable - which to me means breaking even - for the championship run that may still come while this talent pool is together, then I'm going to do everything in my power to keep it going."

Although the Jazz couldn't reach the NBA's promised land, *Financial World* estimated the value of the franchise in 1996 at $145 million, making it the NBA's sixth-most valuable club. It also had the 12th best revenue stream.

Even more, the value of the Jazz had tripled in value since 1991 and was worth seven times Miller's purchase price.

Those were impressive numbers considering Salt Lake City is the NBA's smallest market (according to population) and the second smallest TV market.

That's a costly figure. In 1994-95, the Jazz earned $16.2 million in media revenue compared to the New York Knicks' $25.5.

"The advantages include that you don't have to compete with other professional franchises," Frank Layden told the *Deseret News*. "The disadvantages are that you will never be able to realize the kind of money a New York or Los Angeles team will be able to command."

Salt Lake City commanded international attention during the 1997 NBA finals. It also came under attack from outsiders. Dennis Rodman, the Chicago Bulls power forward and theologian, profanely mocked the Mormon religion.

And Jay Leno was as subtle as ever:

- "Utah fans are very nice, they're very polite people, lovely people. But a lot of them were really upset (after losing the first two games in Chicago). In fact, it was reported after the loss last night, an Osmond was heard to say: 'Darn it.' "
- "Jazz fans were distraught. In fact, I heard half the Osmond family went to bed without flossing."
- "Tonight's tribute to Dennis Rodman by the Mormon Tabernacle Choir has been canceled ...Maybe they'll wash his mouth out with soap."

Rodman appeared with Leno, offering an apology of sorts for his abrasive statement, which netted him a $50,000 fine from the NBA.

"With that Mormon thing, I was kind of screwed," he said. "I didn't realize that Mormon was a religion.

"I wasn't ignorant - I just made a human mistake. If Jordan or Stockton had said something, nothing would've happened."

The Jazz reacted characteristically, winning Games Three and Four at the Delta Center, as did their fans, who reached decibel levels rarely touched before.

In 1997, *Sports Illustrated* asked one representative from each of the 29 NBA teams to name the hottest arena. Chicago's United Center won with eight votes, but the Delta Center was second - and first in the West - with six. No other team got more than two votes.

"It's an absolutely crazy place to play," one voter said. "The fans are incredibly supportive and vocal."

But Jazz fans made their ultimate statement in Game

Five of the Western Championship series in Houston. When Stockton hit a three-pointer as time expired, their worst apprehensions evaporated, prompting what US West termed a "major calling event."

"It's similar to what happens if there is a report of an earthquake or something where everyone picks up the phone," a spokesman said.

Hours later, 15,000 fans greeted the Jazz at the airport.

On its editorial page, the *Deseret News* said: "More than a decade ago, Larry Miller believed Utah was ready for big-time sports and that the state's cherished values and the attributes of a successful modern team are not mutually exclusive.

"Miller had little reason to believe in those days. But his willingness to spend money on a dream saved the state from the ignominy of losing a franchise and it made possible a championship series in a modern arena where cheers will ring with pride.

"It was just one shot, but Stockton's game-winner against Houston Thursday night was so much more. It was a source of pride for the entire state of Utah and for the people - players, owner and fans - who have believed. Basketball is just a game, but it is so much more. And things will never be quite the same in Utah again."

Chapter Eight

Jerry's World

When the NBA season ends, Miami Heat Coach Pat Riley starts working the American lecture circuit, where his motivational speeches on the art of success are as slick as his raked-back hair and $1,000 Armani suits.

He quotes from ancient theoreticians like Sun Tzu, and modern ones like himself, as laid out in *The Winner Within*, his *New York Times* best-seller.

Riley even has a web-site, which advertises him as "America's Greatest Motivational Speaker."

Jerry Sloan, meanwhile, spends summers on his Illinois farm, where, in ancient jeans and a John Deere cap, he methodically plows through each day like the one before.

Wanting the life of Riley is beyond anything that matters to Sloan, whose old-school values are strikingly out of sync with the hip-hop 90s. That life has little appeal as well to Karl Malone and John Stockton, who share their coach's plowhorse ways.

"These guys could only play for a coach like Sloan. Sloan was them and they are Sloan," University of Utah coach Rick Majerus said.

"A team is a reflection of its coach and the Jazz are a reflection of Jerry Sloan," Chicago Bulls GM Jerry Krause said. "They're tough, they're nasty, they're competitive."

More than six dozen coaches have come and gone since Sloan took over the Jazz in 1988. Houston's Rudy Tomjanovich was the only other NBA coach with more than six seasons with his current team at the end of the 96-97 season.

The Jazz has never won fewer than 47 games in a season and finished lower than third in the division in Sloan's tenure. His teams have won four Midwest Division championships, two Western Conference championships and made a respectable run at the Chicago Bulls in back-to-back Finals showdowns.

The secret of Sloan's enduring success?

His sameness. It might be his genius too.

Game after game, year after year, Sloan uses the same conservative half-court attack, the same substitution patterns, the same plays, the same pre-game speeches - the same old, same old.

Monotony works.

"We're not that complicated," Sloan said. "We just believe there's a certain way you have to play to win."

So does Malone, who has followed the Sloan Way to

the top.

Sloan was four, the youngest of 10 children, when his father died, leaving his mother to support the entire family. Malone was three when his father committed suicide, leaving his mother to support nine children.

Sloan vented his fury over his father's death on a basketball court. So did Malone.

It wasn't an easy life for either. Sloan hitchhiked 16 miles to school, but only after rising at 4 a.m., to milk the cows. After a full load of classes and sports, he worked on the farm until sundown.

"I always wondered why he was falling asleep in that first class we had together," Bobbye Sloan, his wife, told the *Deseret News*.

"He's a throwback, a blue-collar guy, a dirt farmer," Layden said.

Added Sloan: "I appreciate farming. I think those people work very hard. I have a farm and I've added to it over the years. I like the country. It's where I'll always be, I guess."

Sloan went to the University of Illinois on a scholarship, but quit after a disappointing freshman year. He took a job in an oil refinery, eventually enrolling at Evansville, which he led to two Division II national championships.

The Baltimore Bullets grabbed him in the second round of the 1965 NBA draft. Sloan averaged 5.7 points and nearly four rebounds per game in his rookie season. The Bulls selected him in the 1966 expansion draft.

Shortly after the regular season started, the Bullets asked for Sloan back. "No, a thousand times no," Bulls owner Dick Klein told them. "We're going to keep Jerry. I knock on wood every time I see him."

Over the next 11 years Sloan averaged 14 points and 7.4 rebounds and led the league in hyper-activity.

"Jerry was always an excitable person," Johnny Kerr, who played with Sloan in Baltimore and coached him in Chicago, explained in *Stockton to Malone!* "I roomed with him in Baltimore on occasion. We'd play a game and I'd go out for a couple of drinks and a sandwich. I'd come back at maybe one, two o'clock in the morning.

"I'd have the light off and be taking off my jacket. I'd see this glow of a cigarette in the dark. Jerry would be sitting up on the other bed and he'd say, 'Red, remember that play in the third quarter?' I'd be getting ready for bed. I'd already had a couple of beers and I'd forgotten about what happened in the third quarter because there was another game tomorrow. But he was so intense he wanted to know why we did certain things in certain situations.

"That really impressed me and when I learned I was coming to Chicago as the coach, I knew he was gonna be one of the players I'd take in the expansion draft. He didn't get a lot of playing time with the Bullets, but I saw him every day in practice. Nobody wanted any part of him. I knew the intensity he had."

Sloan was the first NBA player to volunteer to take a charge on a regular basis. In fact, there was little Sloan wouldn't do, even if meant sacrificing his body on a head-first dive into the front row for a loose ball. Not surprisingly, he wasn't intimidated by the stars. One night, for example, Sloan bounced a ball off Jerry West's face.

"Jerry's the toughest guy I've ever seen," Krause said.

"When I was coming to Chicago, Johnny Kerr told me, 'You're kind of like a spring that's been wound too tight. You might just fly all over the place. You don't want to get that wound up,' " Sloan said.

"I worked hard on not trying to get that way. But I had those tendencies. That's the only way I could compete. I wasn't good enough, in my mind, unless I maintained a high level of intensity.

"When I left Baltimore, I didn't know if I'd be able to play in this league or not. I was drafted fairly high, but I didn't play much in Baltimore and started to have doubts. Two weeks before I went to Chicago, my brother shot himself. I had gotten myself mentally ready to play. But I was concerned because I hadn't worked out for a week because of my brother's funeral. Fortunately, I was in great shape. I could play hard in every minute in training camp and I got a little confidence."

All the hard work paid off: Sloan was a two time All-Star, a six-time All-Defense selection and the Bulls hoisted his jersey to the ceiling when he retired after the 1975-76 season.

Sloan was named coach at the University of Evansville, his alma mater. But he had an inexplicable change of heart five days later and resigned to become a Bulls' assistant.

A few months later, the Evansville team and coaching staff went down in a plane crash. All aboard were killed, including Sloan's replacement, Bobby Watson, who had survived a 31-month tour of Vietnam and earned five Purple Hearts.

"It comes across my mind every morning I go to work," Sloan says.

After three years as an aide, Sloan became the Bulls head coach in 1979-80. He guided them to a 30-52 record and a tie for third place in the Midwest Division.

In 1980-81 the Bulls had a 45-37 record, finished tied for second in the Central Division, beat the New York Knicks 2-0 in a first-round playoff series and then were swept by the Boston Celtics in the semis.

Sloan lasted 51 games of his third season, winning 19 before Rod Thorn gave him the boot.

The problem was Sloan's intensity. It made him a front-line player, but undid him as a coach.

"You have to have intensity to a certain point," Sloan said in *Stockton to Malone!* "But it can be very damaging to you. The intensity I had as a player, it was hard to put aside as a coach. Early in my career, questions from other people seemed to be more of a challenge than anything else. I probably took it that way. That was very difficult for me. I wanted everything to be perfect. I didn't realize that it wasn't going to be."

Sloan coached in the CBA and then joined the Utah Jazz as an assistant to Coach Frank Layden. Eighteen games into the 1988-89 season, he took over for Layden.

At the time, coaches were more vulnerable than ever.

In August, 1992, the San Antonio Spurs hired Coach Jerry Tarkanian to take them to the NBA's promised land. Instead, Tarkanian took them into mid-December, when he was fired, after just 20 games, like some office temp.

Houston's Don Chaney was named the NBA's Coach Of The Year in June, 1991, after leading the Rockets to the best regular-season record in the franchise's 24-year history.

Eight months later, without warning, the Rockets cut him loose in mid-season, proving once more that an NBA coach could be a genius, jerk, winner, whiner - anything except irreplaceable.

One reason for the instability is that players matter more. Coaches aren't the show, they're the sideshow. In 1991-92 in New Jersey, Nets Coach Bill Fitch told Derrick Coleman to go into the game. Coleman went into a funk instead. See ya Bill.

"The first guy they look at is the coach," Chuck Person, Spurs forward said. "Then they just change the coaches and tell the new one, 'Maybe you can motivate this $3 million player.' "

Sidney Lowe was only 32 when he became the interim coach of the Minnesota Timberwolves. But he was old and wise enough to realize he was at the mercy of his players, many of whom couldn't be traded because of contractual clauses or salary-cap restrictions.

"If the players aren't doing well, they say, 'Why don't you put someone else in? Why did you put that guy in?' "

he said. "It's all directed at the coach in the NBA. More so basketball than in football and baseball. You're more visible."

Added Milwaukee Bucks Coach George Karl: "Basically, a coach is about as important as one starter."

Even when a coach climbs the mountaintop, he's apt to stumble off the edge. Chuck Daly won two NBA titles with Detroit, slipped a bit and was gone. Cotton Fitzsimmons took the Phoenix Suns from the ashes of a drug scandal to the top, then joined the suits in the front office. In 1990 Riley left the Lakers in near disrepute, despite having won four NBA championships.

"Sometimes coaches just wear out their welcome," said Washington Wizards Coach Bernie Bickerstaff, who wore out his welcome in Denver and Seattle. "It's not like a college team where you get a transition every four years. Sometimes, as a coach, you get tired of their bull. And they get tired of listening to you. Six or seven years is a lot to be in one place in professional athletics."

Of course, the bottom line also undermines coaches.

"If you don't win, you lose your audience," Phil Jackson said. "The money goes to the winners. The money is what counts. It's not like college, where you have faithful supporters no matter what. It's instant gratification.

"You have a guy like Tarkanian who's been a successful coach for 20 years. And he doesn't even make the all-star break. That says something right there."

Daly almost didn't survive to lead the Pistons to the

NBA's promised land.

"I'd been with the Pistons for a couple years, and we were going through a 4-15 stretch," he said. "I was going to be fired every night. But then we turned it around and won a big home game and won 23 of 27. Same coach. Same players. Same teams. A little patience was shown, and it turned out pretty good for everyone. Stability is as important as anything else. It works."

The instability reached absurd levels when the Minnesota Timberwolves picked Phil Saunders to replace Bill Blair in December, 1995. It was the fifth coaching change in six seasons. "Ridiculous," conceded VP Kevin McHale.

"Embarrassing," added guard Doug West.

Blair, hired before the 1994-95 season, joined Bill Musselman, Jimmy Rodgers and Lowe in the Wolves' trash can.

"If they could fire the players, they would. But they can't," forward Tom Gugliotta said.

Even in the old days, before Generation X, coaches were at the mercy of 22-year-olds with large egos and colossal problems.

Marvin Barnes drove his coaches around the bend, and into early retirement. After he'd missed the Spirits of St. Louis New York-to-Norfolk flight, Barnes was told by Coach Bob MacKinnon to catch the next flight or face dire consequences.

Barnes missed the next three. By the time he arrived at LaGuardia for the next flight, there was none. A bit panicky, he chartered his own flight.

Just before game-time, as MacKinnon spoke to his players, Barnes burst through the locker door wearing a big wide-brimmed hat and a floor-length $10,000 mink coat with a bag of McDonald's hamburgers and french fries in hand.

Barnes peeled off his coat, revealing his Spirits uniform. "Have no fear, BB is here," he proclaimed.

Another night, after scoring 48 points in a losing effort against San Diego, Barnes talked to play-by-play man Bob Costas about the Spirits.

"Bro, you know what's wrong with this team? We don't have any team play. We don't care about each other."

"I thought, 'Maybe Marvin is starting to see what the problem is - this team has no unity,' " Costas recalled.

But Marvin wasn't finished.

"Let me give you an example. Tonight, had 48 points with two minutes to go. Did anybody pass me the ball so I could get 50? Huh? No, they just kept the ball to themselves and I got stuck at 48. Stuff like that; that's what's wrong with these guys."

Another night, Barnes' antics sent another St. Louis coach, Joe Mullaney, into a fit of despair. "He's killing me, he's killing me," Mullaney said over and over.

Sometimes coaches self-destruct. Buffalo Braves Coach Dolph Schayes was furious at his team's inability to handle a halfcourt press. "You guys can't even handle the press," he screamed during halftime. "This is how they're pressing, so this is what we're going to do."

Schayes drew a diagram on the backboard, stared at it, stared some more, and kept staring at it - without saying a word - for several minutes. His players headed back onto the court as Schayes continued to stare wordlessly at the blackboard, frozen in his own thoughts.

In 1979, LA Lakers assistant Paul Westhead became head coach when Jack McKinney suffered a head injury during a bicycling accident.

The Lakers won the NBA title in Westhead's first season, but after Magic Johnson went down with a knee injury, they struggled in his second.

In Westhead's third season, Magic revolted.

"Paul Westhead was a former English professor who'd specialized in Shakespeare," Johnson wrote in *My Life*. "He had coached at LaSalle College before coming to the Lakers, but he didn't have much experience in the pros. Although he tried to motivate us, he wasn't a very good communicator. He spoke in such a complicated manner that there were times when nobody really understood what he was talking about.

"At one point during Westhead's first season with the Lakers, we were down by a point or two with just a few seconds left. During the time-out he looked at me and recited a line from Macbeth: 'If it were done when 'tis done, then 'twere well / It were done quickly.' Say what? But we had been here before, so I made an educated guess: 'Coach, are you saying you want me to get it into the Big Fella?' "

"He nodded. While Westhead didn't usually go around

quoting Shakespeare, there were plenty of times when we didn't have a clue as to what he was saying. But the problem wasn't Westhead's language. The problem was that he violated one of the fundamental rules of sports, politics, business, and just about everything else: 'If it ain't broke, don't fix it.' "

Instead of sticking to the fan-friendly "Showtime" attack, Westhead went to a half-court scheme that alienated some players, Magic most of all. Tensions began to mount. In Salt Lake City, on Nov. 18, Johnson and Westhead got in an argument on the bench. After the game, Westhead pulled Johnson into an equipment room.

''I'm tired of your (bad) attitude," Magic wrote in *My Life*. "And I'm not going to put up with it anymore. Either you start listening to me, or you don't have to play."

"I'm tired of it too," I said, "So maybe you shouldn't play me at all. I'm not doing much anyway, so why don't you send me somewhere else?"

Guess who won that power struggle?

Within days, Westhead was out and Riley was in.

When he handed over the Jazz job to Sloan, Layden said, "Don't overcoach."

Sloan guided the Jazz to a 40-25 record in his first season, and 51-31 overall, counting Layden's record. He also earned the trust of Malone and Stockton, who appreciated his uncommonly short practices. They appreciated it even more in 1990-91, when the Jazz made a slow start, which Sloan attributed it to an exhausting trip to Tokyo at the start of the regular season.

For 18 days the Jazz didn't practice, which allowed players to re-set their body clocks.

"I don't screw around in practice, I'll tell you that," Sloan said in *Stockton to Malone!* "I never played for a coach who practiced over an hour and 15 minutes. I couldn't sit there that long. I figured if I worked hard for an hour and 15 minutes, that's enough, if you put enough energy into it.

"That includes stretching and running and loosening up. I've never had long practices. Maybe in training camp, we had to talk and listen to all the b.s. to start with.

"This is a long drawn-out process to me. I want those guys to have long careers. That wouldn't be fair to John Stockton, Karl Malone and those guys. Their career is more important than mine. I think it's important that you respect that with your players. That's why I've tried to keep them a long time."

Sloan also believes in calling plays, even though Stockton has a couple of advanced degrees in Strategic Hoops.

"It's like he has a computer in him that reacts quicker than anybody else," Frank Layden said, referring to Stockton's exceptional playmaking skills.

"He always knows exactly where to go with the ball and how to get it there," Sloan said.

Other players might have chafed at such an intrusion. In Philadelphia, for example, they said Charles Barkley didn't really recognize the existence of a coach. To the

Round Mound of Rebound, Coach Jim Lynam was just a minor functionary.

To Stockton, Sloan is a major asset.

"It's follow the leader. He's been here, so everybody respects him. When he says something, it happens, or we make it happen," he said.

Added Sloan: "I've always called plays. I don't know if that's right or not. Everybody's entitled to their own opinion. I've always felt like with John, he likes to know where everybody is on the floor. Sometimes if you don't call plays, you play a little bit helter-skelter; I think that takes away from his effectiveness.

"Plus, I've always subscribed to the idea that if a guy's a 50 percent shooter, I like for him to have the ball more than a 30-percent shooter. Sometimes if you call a certain play, you know the ball is gonna go to that position. Now, you have to react to that if the opponent double teams or something. The guys have always accepted the fact that I call plays."

They've also embraced Sloan's system. In 1995-96, Malone and Stockton were the only two players remaining on the Jazz' roster from 1992. Yet newcomers Chris Morris, Greg Foster and Howard Eisley each enjoyed their best NBA seasons.

In 1994-95, the Jazz lost starting center Felton Spencer to an Achilles injury after only 34 games. Forward David Benoit went down with an ankle injury for a month and took another month to return to peak form. Sloan also had to lean on newcomers Antoine Carr and Adam Keefe, who were considered marginal players at best only 12 months before.

Yet Sloan guided the Jazz to 60 wins and improved his eight-year record to 364-193. No team approached the Jazz' efficiency ratings on offense and defense.

"He's been a terrific coach, perhaps one of the most underrated coaches to come along," Los Angeles Lakers Coach Del Harris said in 1998. "His teams play with precision, pride and intensity. They do a really good job of staying the course. Only five years ago, people said his style was boring and dull and couldn't ever win anything, that Stockton and Malone were great but couldn't be championship-caliber guys because they didn't have a dominating center. Well, everybody was wrong."

Added Rudy Tomjanovich: "He definitely doesn't get his due. Jerry's been a great leader for the team and he does it the right way: He doesn't make himself the focal point."

When Wes Unseld coached the Washington Wizards, no one questioned a strategic move to his face because of his commanding presence.

Sloan has some of that coercive charm.

"Nobody fights with Jerry because you know the price would be too high," Layden said. "You might come out a winner, at his age, you might even lick him, but you'd lose an eye, an arm. Everything would be gone in the process."

Sloan could've lost his job a couple times. In 1989-90, Utah won 55 games but lost to Phoenix in the first round of the playoffs. In '91, Sloan's team lost to Portland (4-1) in the Western Conference semifinals after a 54-win regular season.

The Jazz finished the 1991-92 regular season with a 55-27 record, beat the Los Angeles Clippers and Seattle in the first two rounds of the playoffs, then lost the Western Conference finals to Portland in six games.

The following season, Utah won 47 games and lost to Seattle in the first round. In 1993-94 the Jazz was 53-29, barely got by Denver in the second round, then fell to Houston 4-1 in the Conference championship series.

In 1994-95, after a 60-win regular season, the Jazz lost a first-round playoff series to Houston, the low point in Sloan's tenure.

But Malone rushed to his aid.

"Jerry is doing the things now that I'd always hoped he'd do," Malone said. "He'll still get in your face, but he'll also sit down on the bench and watch the game. It seems to me that he's enjoying the game more than he ever has.

"This is the best I've ever seen him coach with a loss and a win. And now I can touch him on the shoulder during a game and he'll kind of smile at me sometimes, whereas in the past, he'd look at me like: 'What are you thinking about?' It's sort of neat to see him like that. He's still intense, now, without a doubt. We got a motto: Once you suit up, you're ready to play. So he's intense, but he also knows when to slack up too."

Malone's support didn't end there. During a rough stretch in March, 1997, he harshly criticized fans who'd criticized Sloan. Rumors of P.J. Carlesimo's imminent firing in Portland fueled the fire.

"It's tough to sit back, with what he's done for this team, and listen to that," Malone said. "(Jerry's) the captain of this ship. You know what the amazing thing is? It's that people won't miss him until he's gone. And then they'll get somebody in here more concerned with wearing $5,000 suits and what car he's driving than whether he wins or not, then we'll miss old Jerry."

Added Bobbye, Sloan's wife: "He's been criticized his whole life. He's the youngest of 10 kids in the family that had a definite pecking order. But the time it came to his turn, it was like 'shut up.' Even if he did good, he didn't know it. So, he's not on a pedestal, he's never full of himself."

A year later, when the Jazz appeared to balk at extending Sloan's contract, Malone warned: Do it or lose me.

"I know my coach," Malone said. "I read my coach really well. I can tell when he's not the coach I know. I can tell when something is on his mind. He's not going to say that he's distracted, but I can tell that he is. What's happening between Jazz management and coach Sloan is b.s.

"I respect him as a coach and for being the kind of man he is. A lot of people sometimes think he is too hard, but I know I need that. Although sometimes he doesn't know when to pull back. But I accept that in him. I accept his desire to win."

Sloan's salary of $1.25 million made him the NBA's 23rd highest paid coach in 1998.

At the start of the 1997-98 season, Rick Pitino, Larry Brown, Pat Riley, Chuck Daly, John Calipari, Lenny Wilkens, Mike Fratello and Phil Jackson each were making at least $3 million per year.

It appeared the NBA was becoming a coach's league.

"Maybe it's sending a message a little bit and letting the players and everybody know this person is going to be there for a while; that there will be a singular voice that will lead them," Riley said.

"You eat, drink and breathe the game with (players). I think coaches should be the one who should have a lot to say. These contracts send the message that owners want someone to be in charge. There is nothing wrong with that in today's age.

"I think it's long overdue."

Doug Collins, who lost his job with the Detroit Pistons after a player revolt, also endorsed the trend.

"The team is (saying): 'This guy is the coach, and if there are changes, maybe it's going to be player-wise, not coach-wise.' "

At the same time, during the heart of the '97-98 season, Sloan's wife was battling breast cancer. She felt pain in her left breast in June, '97, the night the Jazz lost to the Chicago Bulls in Game Six of the NBA Finals. She didn't tell her family at first, preferring instead to learn the extent of the cancer.

Once she did, she began chemotherapy treatments

that lasted into the '97-98 season, then underwent reconstructive breast surgery on Jan. 2, while the Jazz were in the middle of a seven-game winning streak.

Sloan didn't tell his team or staff.

"(But) we've noticed a big change in him as a coaching staff, from the standpoint of being more settled at practice," assistant coach Kenny Natt said. "Last year, every day, it was something. All the way up to the last game of the season, in the Finals, we had confrontations and things out on the floor, whereas now, he's not after every guy.

"The thing that happened to his wife made him realize there's more to life. That has settled him down. The players have sensed it. Last year, he was more at guys all the time, really going after them, and it had them on edge and they were going crazy."

The illness compelled him to re-examine the plane crash that killed the Evansville team as it left Indiana for a game in Tennessee.

Bobbye went public with her illness in the February issue of the Jazz *Homecourt* magazine. At the same time, Sloan wondered aloud about his status with the club.

"In many ways," he said, "this has been the toughest year of my life. On the other hand, it's been the most rewarding year of my life."

After the 1997-98 season, the Jazz and Sloan quietly agreed to a new three-year deal.

"We have two of the greatest players at their positions because of Jerry Sloan," Frank Layden said. "I don't know of anybody else who could take our team to the next level and do it the way we want to do it. We haven't paid the devil to get to the next level.

"Jerry's a blue-collar guy. These people identify with Jerry. They like how he is."

Sloan was unavailable for comment. Instead, he was tending to more than 600 acres of grain, collecting old furniture, tinkering with his tractor, in McLeansboro, Illinois.

The same-old, same-old.

Chapter Nine

The Lost Years

Being Charles Barkley is not an easy job.

Day shifts, night shifts, weekends, holidays – the bellicose forward is one of America's hardest working icons.

Why not?

Hard work has made Barkley a living museum.

He can play with the best of 'em, quip with the best of 'em, market himself with the best of 'em and self-destruct with the best of 'em.

Barkley was doing the latter in the 1991-92 season.

With little concern for consequences, he insulted teammates, ownership, fans and anyone else who blocked his bleak path. He hit bottom in Milwaukee, where he was arrested and charged with misdemeanor battery after punching a Bucks' fan.

By the time the Philadelphia 76ers reached Salt Lake City, Barkley was running out of profanities

"If you're not having fun in this game, it's time to give

it up," he said. "I'm not having any fun."

The Mailman did his best to lighten Barkley's load. After the Jazz beat the Sixers 100-94, Malone wrapped the burly forward in a big bear hug at the Delta Center and talked to him about his predicament.

"I look at Charles and see a guy who's not only unhappy that he hasn't won, but a guy who really doesn't like the whole situation he's in, the guys he's playing with, the guys who are his bosses. That's not the case with me," Malone said.

But it would be.

In 1994, Malone looked at himself, and saw Barkley, the Barkley of 1992.

"With what's happening now, I see playing .500 ball for the rest of my career," he said "And that's something I don't like. I don't have 10 years left to play in this league. I want to win it in Utah. But if you don't show me as management that you do, I know some teams I want to play for.

"I often say to myself," Malone said, 'What if something happened to Stockton? What if something happened to me? Would we be in the lottery?' David Robinson says the reason's he's playing better this season is because he doesn't have to worry about getting all the rebounds. I wish I could have that luxury. I guess I'll never know what that'll be like."

Winning a championship would have appeased Malone, but Utah couldn't even gain admittance to a championship series, much less win one.

The Jazz had come of age in the 80s, when the Lakers' Showtime attack was in full bloom. Bad timing.

When the Lakers finally ran out of gas, the Jazz started bumping itself off, blowing three playoff series in the first round.

More bad timing.

There were several theories for the annual meltdown: The Jazz was too predictable; too dependent on Malone and Stockton; lacked adequate depth; wasn't athletic enough; had trouble matching up against smaller lineups; didn't have a winning attitude.

It didn't end there.

According to Chuck Person, the Jazz would never win a title because Malone "…will back down in pressure situations."

"Utah has been known to crumble at the end," added San Antonio forward Terry Cummings.

Those accusations inflamed Malone, especially the one from Person, an accomplished trash talker.

"I'll cut him up on the court very quickly," he said. "Every year, we have a winning team, and that's important. Can Chuck Person say that? No! If you read newspaper clippings, I always have guys taking a stab at me. I'll sum it up by saying that I have more class than Chuck Person."

But Malone didn't have a championship ring and, with each playoff meltdown, he descended into a deeper funk. A Dream Team career was turning into a nightmare.

"People will always consider you a loser until you are

(a champion)," Coach Jerry Sloan said. "That's just the way it is."

No one knows that better than Minnesota Vikings quarterback Fran Tarkenton, who earned a spot in football infamy with an 0-3 Super Bowl record.

"Losing the Super Bowl is the ultimate humiliation," he said. "There is no consolation of any kind. People ridicule and abuse you."

"You feel a certain pity or sorrow for guys, who don't play on great teams," ex-Pittsburgh Steelers quarterback Terry Bradshaw added. "There are a lot of great quarterbacks who can put up a lot of stats. But the bottom line is that when you get in the big games, you win those suckers. You've got to win a championship because that's what it's all about.

"When you're all done, they say, 'Look Bub, I know you threw for 400,000 yards and 500 touchdowns, but how many rings do you have?'"

The pressure to get a ring is enough to make grown men choke.

In the 1995 NBA playoffs alone:

• The Knicks led the Pacers by six points with 18 seconds left in the opening game of their Eastern Conference series. In quick succession Anthony Mason threw away an inbounds pass, John Starks blew a couple of free throws, and Patrick Ewing missed a 10-footer. The Pacers won.

• Vlade Divac missed two free throws in the final moments of regulation play and the Lakers lost in overtime to San Antonio.

• Sean Elliott, an 80-per cent shooter from the line, blew two free throws in the final seconds that cost the Spurs a win against the Rockets.

• Michael Jordan's sloppy ball-handling and poor decision-making cost the Bulls a victory against Orlando.

• Even a referee choked. Before the opening game of the Houston-Phoenix series, veteran Jake O'Donnell refused to shake hands with Rockets star Clyde Drexler. In the second quarter, he whistled Drexler for a dubious call, then ejected him when Drexler protested the call. The NBA, concerned about the pair's on-going feud, never allowed O'Donnell to ref again.

"I remember my first couple years in the league, when I wasn't in the playoffs and thinking, 'Oh, it's not that big a difference,' " Tom Chambers told *Sport.* "Then when I got into it my first time around, I was shell-shocked. It's a completely different thing."

Added Starks: "If you don't go into the playoffs knowing that they're nothing like the regular season, it's already too late. By the time you figure it out, you'll already be on the plane ride home."

Young players are especially clueless. Before Utah's 1998 Western Conference finals series against the Los Angeles Lakers, Jazz broadcaster Rod Hundley, an All-Star from the Lakers glory years, said "(The Lakers) have more talent than anybody in the league, but they're too Hollywood to me. They're not very organized. They're like the Globetrotters, everybody doing their own thing.

"I think Del Harris is a good coach. But I don't think he has control of the team. I don't know if anybody can control that team."

To rouse his players, Harris read Hundley's critique to them, then waited for an angry response. He didn't get one; he didn't get any response. The Lakers had never heard of Hundley.

The regular season resembles post-season like Roy Marble resembles Michael Jordan. Like not at all. What are the differences?

• More preparation time. When he coached Seattle, Bernie Bickerstaff took the Sonics to Colorado Springs to prepare for a playoff series against the Denver Nuggets. He wanted them to acclimate themselves to the altitude as well as isolate them from distracting influences. In 1997 he took his Washington team to a retreat in West Virginia.

The New York Knicks and Miami Heat also went on pre-playoff retreats, where they studied their opponents with the fervor of grad students. Every playoff team hits the books. "We scouted 37 (Houston) Rockets games," Minnesota coach Flip Saunders told *Sports Illustrated*. "In those games Hakeem touched the ball 480 times when he wasn't double-teamed and then shot the ball 460 times. There were about 375 times when Olajuwon was double-teamed and he shot the ball only 128 times."

Whew.

Traditionally, the Bulls unite via a self-imposed gag order. They talk only reluctantly with the media and during their 90-minute weight-lifting sessions total silence is required.

• Different strategy. Golden State Coach Don Nelson stunned the Jazz in 1989 by "going small." He isolated a smaller but quicker player against the bigger Jazz, then exploited the matchup with an end-to-end offense and half-court trap press. He also moved 7-foot-7 center Manute Bol to the top of the key, where he lured Utah's big men from their natural positions. Bol threw in several three-pointers to boot.

"Nellie's got the Jazz so screwed up they don't know what they're doing," an NBA referee told *Sports Illustrated.*

• Familiarity breeds insights. The Sonics' trapping, rotating defense bedeviled opponents during the regular season. But during the 1997 playoffs, the Phoenix Suns made the Sonics pay for their predictability.

• Role players. Two stars aren't enough. You need backup talent. Ask Jordan and Pippen or Olajuwon and Drexler.

• Playoff games are rougher and slower. Larry Brown was astounded after his San Antonio Spurs were manhandled. "It's a horror film watching the way David Robinson got beat up in our playoff series with Golden State. I know everybody talks about it getting physical, but Coach (Dean) Smith wrote me and said he's never seen a mugging like that. But if they let you do it, they let you do it.

"You just have to learn to adjust. Your players have to go through it; coaches have to go through it. Michael

(Jordan) said it best after he won it all (for the first time): 'It's been seven long years.' It's not a process that happens overnight."

Adjusting *quickly* from regular season to play-off intensity is, well, absolutely necessary. Otherwise, you're out - *fast.*

The first-round flubs were especially galling to the Mailman, including:

• In 1988, the Jazz staggered the Lakers with a 28-point blowout win in Game Six of a Western Conference semi-final series, then lost the decisive seventh game.

• In 1992, Stockton was sidelined with an eye injury shortly before halftime in Game Five in Portland. He couldn't return, the Blazers won in overtime then took the series in Game Six.

• In 1993, the Jazz lost in five games to the Supersonics despite a half-time lead in the fifth game.

After the 1993 defeat, Miller vowed to keep Malone and Stockton for the long haul. A gesture of loyalty? Or proof only profits mattered?

Malone, who'd threatened a contract holdout in pre-season, feared the worst, and told Miller so in a private meeting. He went public at the 1994 All-Star game.

"This team isn't committed to winning," he said. "They gotta prove it to me by attempting to sign players or something to win and not just players out of the CBA and stuff like that. My whole thing is that I hate to hear, 'I'm trying. We're trying.'

"Why is it now that we're trying and everybody else is

doing. That's my attitude. I'm frustrated with the trying part of it, instead of going out and actually doing it."

Frank Layden, Malone's No. 1 booster, wasn't that day.

"We can't even fulfill his needs just by paying him money," he said. "Now we have to promise him a championship."

But after the all-star game, Miller promptly acquired guard Jeff Hornacek, heaping all the pressure on Malone's shoulders.

It showed in the playoffs. After the Jazz gained a 3-0 lead over the Denver Nuggets in a Western Conference semifinal series, Malone made a startling announcement.

"If I win the ring this year," he said, "I have no reason to play anymore. Financially, you know, I'm secure for life. I love to play this game, but I don't like a lot of the other stuff."

"I don't blame him," Sloan added. "I'd like to retire too, but I still have to eat."

The pressure split and cracked the Jazz at a moment of maximum stress. In the first half of Game Five against Denver, as Malone struggled to find his game, Miller pleaded with Sloan to bench his No. 1 scorer.

Near the start of the second half, Miller got in a shoving match with two Nuggets fans.

"I was really scared," one of those fans said. "It was behavior unbecoming to an NBA owner. This wasn't just some drunken out-of-control fan. This was the *owner* of an NBA team."

After the game, which the Jazz lost in two overtimes,

Malone appeared dumbfounded.

"I don't really know what went on," said the Mailman, who finished with 22 points and 13 rebounds before fouling out in the first overtime. "But he can do whatever he wants. He's the owner. There are not a lot of people I count on in this business. When it gets tough, anybody will turn on you. If he said to bench me, it's his team. It's his thing."

It wasn't Miller's first blow-up. During a March 14 game against the Lakers, Miller ran on the court during a scuffle between Stockton and Lakers center Elden Campbell.

"I told him to pick on somebody his own size," Miller said.

Stockton appreciated Miller's support, as did his teammates. But the Game Five incident was a different matter.

"I don't even want to talk about it," Malone told reporters the following day. "When's all said and done, there will be time to talk."

Malone insisted the blow-up wouldn't interfere with his game.

"Let me tell you something: I respect Larry. I always have, I always will. I'm not concerned with him right now. He's the furthest thing from my mind right now, like a lot of other people."

The flap staggered the Nuggets.

"I don't know that what the owner does affect them," Nuggets Coach Dan Issel said. "I'd feel a whole lot more comfortable if John Stockton or Jeff Hornacek or someone else was up in the stands trying to choke somebody. Then you might say 'some cracks are showing.'

"I know Karl is a true professional. If there were words between him and Miller, that will only help Karl's performance."

Utah's problems intensified in Game Six, which the Nuggets won 94-91 to tie the series at three games. When asked about the team's mood, Malone lashed out.

"What do you think? You think we're (expletive) quitters? What do you think the mood of the team is?"

"We're running out of time," Frank Layden said. "We're becoming like the other teams."

In Game Seven, however, the Mailman delivered the goods. He scored 10 points in the first quarter - on 5-for-6 shooting, and 22 points in the first half. He finished with 31 points, 12 rebounds, six assists and two steals. And as the final seconds ticked away, he wagged a finger in Dikembe Mutombo's face.

He wept a few minutes later.

"It was a humongous win for us," Malone said. "I just want to thank God for giving me the strength to go out and play hard. The court is my sanctuary. When bad things happen, that's the one place I go."

Miller and the NBA had "mutually decided" he would not watch the two final games at the Delta Center. Instead, the Jazz owner listened to the play-by-play broadcast in his Falcon convertible, which he considered his sanctuary.

"Larry, if you're listening, I have the utmost respect for you and when the season is over, maybe we'll get together to fish and talk," said Malone, when interviewed in the post-game radio broadcast.

Next on tap for the Jazz: Hakeem Olajuwon's Houston Rockets.

"Out of the frying pan into the fire," Malone said.

Malone almost went into the hospital. Crippled by a severe flu bug, he and the Jazz were blown away in five games, which intensified their discord and sense of omen about the future.

Although stories about a trade involving Malone became hot copy in the off-season, nothing materialized. When the Mailman reported to training camp, the Jazz lineup included several new faces, including center Felton Spencer and free-agent forwards Adam Keefe and Antoine Carr. The civil war of '94 was forgotten.

The Jazz won 60 games, a notable feat since Spencer went down with a torn Achilles tendon in January.

Utah's first-round opponent was the Houston Rockets, winners of 47 games during a tumultuous regular season.

In February, Houston Coach Rudy Tomjanovich traded power forward Otis Thorpe to Portland for Clyde Drexler, which set in motion Vernon Maxwell's departure. As the playoffs neared, Olajuwon was sidelined for two weeks with anemia. In other words, it appeared the Rockets were in a state of disarray.

But after falling behind the Jazz 2-1 in the five-game series, they found their bearings, and advanced to the next round and ultimately another NBA Championship Series, where they won their second straight title.

Despite the staggering blow, Sloan defended his embattled team.

"Just like always, our guys played as hard as they could play," he said. "Two or three years ago, people said we should break up this team and start over again. But our guys are awfully tough. They try to win every night. That's one thing I've always appreciated - one thing that always gives us a chance.

"Not everybody is fortunate enough to win. People who give everything they can give - and people who are tough enough to keep trying - they are special people too."

Sloan knew about close calls. From 1971-75 he played for the Chicago Bulls, who averaged 54 wins per season, yet failed to make a championship appearance. In 1975, the Bulls won a Midwest Division title and advanced to the Western Conference finals, where they took a 3-2 lead over Golden State.

But the Warriors won the final two games, then swept the Washington Bullets in the finals.

Sloan went into a deep funk, an experience he wouldn't permit himself to endure in later years with the Jazz.

"We've experienced a lot of failures over the years," he said in *Stockton to Malone!* "But it takes a lot of pride. You have to have a lot of pride in yourself to keep coming back and trying. I don't think our guys should be criticized for coming back and trying.

"Just because you haven't been successful, I don't think that means you're a bad person ... Are you gonna teach your kid that if you don't win a championship, you're gonna be a failure the rest of your life?"

The Jazz fought off complacency, adding Chris Morris, Greg Foster and Howard Eisley for the 95-96 season. Stockton and Malone were the only players remaining from 1992, when the Jazz went to the conference finals for the first time.

Nevertheless, the Jazz won 55 games, and prepared for another shot at the playoffs. In the first game of the first series, Utah trailed the Portland Trail Blazers by eight points.

Desperate for a quick fix, Sloan sent 12th man Bryon Russell to save the day, which he did with 12 fourth-quarter points.

Russell continued to shine against Portland, then during a 4-2 semifinal victory against San Antonio, which set the Jazz up for a Western Conference championship series against the Seattle Supersonics.

After falling behind 3-1, the Jazz rallied to force a seventh game at Key Arena. After trailing by eight points with 5:29 left, the Jazz rallied to within three points of a title shot.

But Shawn Kemp made four free throws in the final 1:17. Malone missed two with eight seconds remaining and Stockton was uncommonly passive during the stretch run. Usually, Stockton is an expert at the end game, where his self-possession produces baskets or clever passes that lead to baskets at the wire.

"I think they're probably the best in the league at running the half-court game," Bickerstaff said. "Stockton probably has down how much it takes for them to utilize and execute their offense because they've been doing it for so long."

"The clock gets down to 3-2-1 and then all of a sudden Stockton will pull up and make a great shot or whip it to you for an easy bucket," Spencer said. "It's definitely instinctive. It's just in him."

But not in Game Seven.

"I saw Stockton's face at the end," Seattle coach George Karl said. "And there was a hurt there. A very big hurt."

Malone didn't look well himself.

"I'm in this thing for one reason, and that's to win it," he said.

No one doubted Malone's skills in 1996; the NBA selected him one of its top 50 players of all time. But he had nothing to show for it.

Despite his protestations, individual honors matter to Malone, as they do to 100 % of the NBA population. During the early years of the Stockton-Malone era, Jazz players selected Stockton as the team's MVP, which angered Malone. The Jazz discontinued the award.

But the 1996-97 season would be different.

From day one, Malone consistently played at a peak level, bulling his way through double teams, running the floor like a sprinter, taking and giving a beating, hitting the face-up jumper.

Malone didn't let up, and neither did Jazz fans, who began chanting "MVP" at the Delta Center.

Other superstars took up the beat.

"Michael has kept the Bulls there," said former MVP Charles Barkley. "But I think Karl deserves it."

Malone figured his chances were nil. Although he'd averaged 26.1 points and 10.8 rebounds per game in his career, Shawn Kemp had out-polled him by more than 375,000 votes for the starting power forward spot in the '97 All-Star game.

"It has a lot to do with television commercials," Malone said of fan balloting. "If people see your face a lot, and you put up decent numbers, you're set."

Malone finished with a 27.4 point scoring average, which was second only to Jordan. The Jazz finished with a 64-18 record, the Western Conference's best mark, which was a first for the team.

For the first time, the Jazz team, and not just Malone and Stockton, displayed a nasty side in the playoffs, as the L.A. Clippers discovered while being swept in three games.

"I think people throughout the league do look at us a certain way, like we're nice guys who don't like contact or who shy away from playing physical," Malone said. "Well, we've got several guys on this team who can get after it and love to do the physical banging that this time of year is all about. We like it so much now, some might even call us dirty."

During the first game of a second-round series against the Lakers, Malone, Sloan and Antoine Carr were slapped with technicals. Even Jeff Hornacek, a finalist for the NBA's Sportsmanship Award, did some trash talking.

"Maybe some things are different this year," Stockton said.

The Jazz gained a 2-0 lead over the Lakers, but lost to LA in Game Three, due in part to Malone's 2-of-20 shooting.

After his embarrassing performance, Malone phoned his wife for emotional support.

"What's 2-for-20?" she asked.

The Mailman started laughing, shrugged his shoulders, and went to the beach. "In 12 years, I might have left my hotel room five or six times," he said in *Stockton to Malone!* "But this time I just wanted to get out. So I spent my Friday at the beach. I told my wife, and she said: 'You never go for a bike ride.'

"But I guess there comes a time for everything. We saw a guy with all these broken bottles on the ground and he was jumping off a chair right into the bottles. I said, 'And I thought I had a bad day.' "

Malone rebounded in Game Four with 42 points. The Jazz finished off the Lakers in the fifth game, during which Malone's three young children, Kadee Lyunn, Kylee Ann and Karl Jr. held up a sign that read "Daddy MVP/Jazz NBA Champions."

"I don't know where they get those. Maybe they know

something I don't," Malone said.

Maybe, because on the eve of the Western Conference championship series against the Houston Rockets, Malone became the oldest man ever to win the MVP Trophy.

"He's really emerged over the years," Layden said. "Not only as a player, but also as a human being. In an age where we are very critical of our athletes and we have so many problems with them, Karl Malone is a hero."

Added Stockton: "Nothing about him surprises me anymore. He's built on his game every year. He could have stayed pat where he was after the third year. I think he was the best power forward in the league. Every year, he found another way to hurt a team. That's his legacy. He was great and he improved on that when some others might have not."

Malone accepted the trophy during a ceremony preceding the opening tip of Game One, but declined to comment. Later, he put the trophy in a box, in his closet, under a pair of cowboy boots.

He was determined to avoid complacency.

In Game One, Malone missed 15-of-21 shots, though the Jazz managed a 101-86 victory. After four games, the series was tied at two games apiece, and headed back to the Delta Center where Jazz fans went over the top.

"Most hated (fans) in the league," Houston forward Eddie Johnson said as the war of words heated up.

"If you can't take the heckling, get out of the kitchen," Frank Layden said in rebuttal. "You're supposed to be a pro."

The Jazz won 96-91, lifting it to within one victory of a NBA championship showdown with the Chicago Bulls. But the Jazz lacked a KO blow.

It'd taken a 3-0 lead over Denver in '94, a 2-1 lead over Houston in a best-of-five series in '95, a 2-0 lead over Portland in a best-of-five series in '96, and a 3-1 edge over San Antonio in 1996.

And lost the next game each time.

The Jazz was losing its way in Game Six too, falling 13 points behind the Rockets in the fourth quarter. It trailed by 10, 96-86 with three minutes left at The Summit.

"Coach is always saying, 'Never give up, never give up,' " Stockton said. "He convinced us to keep playing."

After a three-pointer by Bryon Russell and a pair of free throws, the Jazz trailed by just five points. "I think that's when we knew we'd win the game," Jeff Hornacek said. "We knew in the end they'd be tight in a close game. We had the luxury of a seventh game, but they didn't."

A few minutes later, Stockton drove by Sedale Threatt for a layup. He stole the ball from Clyde Drexler on Houston's next possession, and scored again on Threatt. With 22 seconds remaining, several Jazz players converged on Drexler, who was forced to throw up a wild bank shot. Malone came down with the rebound.

"Each guy on this team did something special to give us an opportunity," he said.

With the score tied at 100, Coach Jerry Sloan called for - Surprise! - a pick and roll.

Russell inbounded the ball to Stockton with 2.8

seconds left - a split-second after Malone had thrown his massive body in front of Clyde Drexler.

Drexler couldn't begin to get around Malone, Charles Barkley couldn't make the switch, Stockton received the pass, then buried a three-pointer that lifted the Jazz into the NBA Finals. Finally.

"It was the best pick I ever set in my life," Malone said.

In the post-game press conference, the Mailman fielded questions in a brand-new "Western Conference Champions" T-shirt. While describing Stockton's historic shot, one of the NBA's most towering stars walked to the edge of the crowd and shouted:

"Finish it," Hakeem Olajuwon said. "Now finish it."

Chapter Ten

Bulldozed

After years of post-season meltdowns, the Utah Jazz' reputation as a team that couldn't handle the furnace heat of playoff pressure seemed irrevocable.

So when Karl Malone stepped to the free-throw line with a chance to beat the Chicago Bulls with 9.2 seconds left in Game One of the 1997 NBA Finals, he knew he had a chance to beat a bad rap in the process.

So did Scottie Pippen, which is why the Bulls' forward strolled over to Malone.

"The Mailman doesn't deliver on Sundays," he hissed.

Actually, after starting the game by missing seven of his first eight shots, Malone had delivered the Jazz to the brink of victory. Late in the game, he'd made a free throw, two consecutive jumpers, two more free throws and a driving layup. In all, Malone had scored nine of the Jazz' final 12 points in a brassy display of heavy mettle.

So now he stood at the free-throw line, with the ball - and a chance for a little redemption - resting in the palm of his hands.

He blew both of 'em.

A few moments later, Michael Jordan came down and hit another game-winning jumper.

"That's what MVPs do," he said after an 84-82 win.

Ouch!

The only thing more haunting than never playing in an NBA Championship game is losing an NBA Championship game, especially in the final seconds. In fact, championship meltdowns are as much a part of NBA lore as championship triumphs, as Wilt Chamberlain well knows.

Chamberlain's nightmare actually began at Kansas. The Jayhawks' triple-overtime loss to North Carolina in 1957 was an omen that gathered gravity with each passing defeat to Bill Russell's Boston Celtics. Sixteen years later, in his book *Wilt,* Chamberlain, who eventually won two NBA titles, revealed the magnitude of that first wound.

"I've always been more bitter about that loss than any other single game in my whole college and professional career. I guess because that's the game that started the whole 'Wilt's a loser' thing that's been thrown at me for more than 15 years now.

"For most of those years, people have been writing that Kansas was the pre-season favorite to win everything my sophomore year - and my junior year as well - and that we, I, blew it both times. That just isn't true. But people only remember what Phog Allen said when I enrolled at Kansas. He told everyone: 'Wilt Chamberlain's the greatest player I ever saw. With him, we'll never lose a game; we could win the national championship with Wilt, two sorority girls and two Phi Beta Kappas.'

"That was ridiculous of course, but it gave the public an image of me that has endured to this day - an image of Wilt Chamberlain as Superman. A guy who should never lose. So when my team does lose, it must be my fault. Right? I'm not performing up to expectations. Or I'm choking. Or I'm letting Bill Russell psyche me out. Or I'm being selfish."

Jerry West won an NBA title too, but he too is haunted by the ones that got away, especially the 1968-69 finale against the Boston Celtics.

"Distraught wouldn't even have been a good word for it. It was depressing as could be. I couldn't believe we lost to that team that year. I didn't think they were as good as we were. It took me a year-and-a-half to start to get over it.

"I think players are measured by the number of championships they won."

Malone had a couple days to get over his Game One meltdown; Coach Jerry Sloan had a couple days to come up with a way to beat the Bulls.

Sloan had the bigger problem.

"They are the greatest team since the Celtics won 11 in 13 years (from 1957-69)," said Pat Riley, long-time and much-traveled coach in the NBA. "I don't think anybody's going to win until Michael retires. Sometimes you build a great team and you'll never win a championship because you had the misfortune of playing at the same time that Jordan went through his run."

Nonetheless, Riley had developed a theory or two, which he outlined in *Lindy's Pro Basketball* magazine:

• Run away from trouble. A fastbreak will defend a

team against the Bulls' defense. "Make it hard for Jordan, make it hard for Scottie. Rebound defensively and run," Miami point guard Tim Hardaway said.

Added Riley: "If you're not running and rebounding and getting second shots at every opportunity you get, then it's gonna be very difficult to score."

• Literally "attack" them. Get physical. Knock 'em around. Stick a hand in their face. Foul them intentionally, because refs won't call all of 'em.

The problem with plan one is Rodman. If you can't get a rebound, you can't run and Rodman is the rebound king. The problem with plan two is that the Bulls can spread their offense to space out the attackers.

In Game Two, Malone's composure was stretched to the limit. The Bulls management passed out thousands of "clackers" as fans entered the United Center. Ninety seconds into the game, Malone went to the free-throw line for the first time since his Game One travails. Out came the clackers. Once again, Mailman blew both of 'em.

Two minutes later, Malone returned to the line, with the Bulls holding an 8-1 lead. Once more, the United Center turned into a Clackerdome. This time, he made both shots.

But the rout was on, with the Bulls breezing to a 97-85 victory. Jordan was unstoppable, finishing with 38 points, 13 rebounds and nine assists. At the end, fans chanted "MVP, MVP, MVP" - a mocking rebuke to Malone.

Jordan was privately enraged that Malone had won the award. In fact, he used the MVP "slight" to fuel his all-consuming ambition.

"For Michael, it's not just about winning," said former Bulls guard B.J. Armstrong. "It is about being an icon and building a legacy. He wants to do things no one will ever do again. At playoff time he is even better than advertised.

"Unmatched intensity."

The Jazz, meanwhile, had played with no intensity.

"Obviously I'm stinking it up right now," said Malone, who scored 20 points and shot 6-for-20. "We played soft, and how do you argue about that?"

Added Stockton: "I've missed four games in 13 years and after all those nights of tearing my heart out, I've finally got to the show and we're not competing."

But when the series shifted to the Delta Center, so did the character and texture of the series. Not to mention the noise level. During introductions for Game Three, the Bulls were rattled by an ear-splitting combination of firecrackers, exploding balloons, screaming fans and the roaring engine of a Harley Davidson motorcycle - which delivered the Jazz mascot to center court.

"It's a deafening scene," NBC play-by-play man Marv Albert said before the opening tip.

Thousands of fans also watched the game on a giant outdoor screen across the street.

"This is the only show in town and they're with us all the way," center Greg Foster said.

Building on this emotion, the Jazz recorded a 104-93 victory, thanks to a monstrous 37-point, 10-rebound performance from Malone that included 22 points in the first half. Foster scored 15 of his career-high 17 points by intermission.

"The big guys whipped on us tonight," Phil Jackson said.

Before Game Four, Jackson bought some ear plugs for his staff. More importantly, he ratcheted up his defense, which smothered the Jazz at every turn. The Bulls held Malone to 23 points and Hornacek to 13. Stockton had scored only 11 points entering the final quarter.

With 2:42 left, the Bulls led 71-66 and the Jazz hadn't scored a field goal in six minutes. But Stockton hit a three-pointer from five feet beyond the line with 2:32 remaining.

A few moments later, he slapped the ball from Jordan and drove to the basket before getting fouled by Jordan.

Stockton made one of two free throws to cut the lead to three points. He was fouled again shortly after Pippen missed a corner jumper, then made both shots to cut the deficit to 73-72 with 1:01 left.

On the next possession, Jordan drove across the key and put up a 17-footer, which fell short. Stockton grabbed the rebound, took one dribble, then hurled an 80-foot strike over Pippen, Jordan, Tony Kukoc and into the waiting hands of Malone, who took one giant stride and laid in the go-ahead basket.

"I turned up the floor, saw Karl's position and cut it loose," Stockton said. "If you could've suspended time in the middle of the air, Jerry would have probably strangled me."

"I hollered, 'Oh no' at first," Sloan conceded.

But the Jazz hadn't secured a victory yet. With 18 seconds left, Malone went to the free-throw line, the scene of his Game One humiliation. "I normally think about faraway places, but this time I thought about 650 million people watching on TV - again," he said.

Once again, Scottie Pippen tried to rattle him, but Jeff Hornacek put his body between Pippen's and Malone's to cushion the verbal blow. "He kept inching his way over there and I thought he was going to say some more stuff," Hornacek said.

Malone made both free throws this time and the relief was evident in his beaming smile, which grew even brighter when the Jazz walked of the court with a 78-73 victory and the series tied 2-2.

"As a player, when things don't go well, you wish you had another chance. I did."

Added Pippen: "I guess the Mailman delivers on Sundays out there."

Pippen didn't stop there.

"They're giving us everything we can ask for," he said. "Five, six days ago, everyone was predicting that we would sweep this team. Now everything is turned around. It's been very difficult for us. It's more difficult for us than any team we've faced in the finals."

Jordan, who scored 22 points in a flawed performance, was eager to put the loss behind him and focus on Game Five.

"There's gonna be games where I can't live up to the fantasy or hype of what people have built up Michael Jordan to be," he said. "I'm accustomed to living with that."

The Bulls' problems were only beginning. Jordan was too ill to attend a practice on the morning of Game Five, a stunning blow to his teammates, who'd never seen him skip a workout.

They saw him that night, on the locker room floor, fighting off a viral infection, which threatened to keep him on his back.

But Jordan played as well and intensely as ever, especially in the fading moments. With 46 seconds left, he rebounded his own missed free throw, passed to Pippen, then moved to shooting position behind the three-point line. After Pippen passed the ball back to him, Jordan buried the trey with 25 seconds left, lifting the Bulls to a 90-88 win.

Jordan finished with 38 points - but barely.

"I almost played myself into passing out," he said. "I came in and was almost dehydrated and it was all just to win a basketball game. I couldn't breathe."

The Series returned to Chicago where it ended in Game Six. On the final possession, Jordan brought the ball down court, then kicked it over to Steve Kerr, whose trey sealed a 90-86 Bulls win.

One year later, after blowing away the Lakers in the Western Conference Championships, the Jazz had 10 days to prepare for another NBA Finals run at the Bulls.

Malone was rusty from the opening tip of Game One, making just 9-of-25 shots in a display of futility that lasted until late in the game, when he hit twice from the left wing. The second gave the Jazz a four-point lead with 55 seconds left.

Stockton guided the Jazz to an 88-85 win in overtime, but that didn't conceal Malone's passive, ineffective play, which angered many fans.

"What's the pressure on me personally? I don't think you guys even know," he said afterward.

The pressure increased after Game Two, which the Bulls won 93-88. The Bulls' state-of-the-art defense forced the Jazz into an uncharacteristic 20 turnovers, and Malone out of his game. He missed 11-of-16 shots, didn't make a second-half field goal and scored only four points in the final half and 16 overall.

After two games, Malone was 14-of- -41 from the field and 3-of-21 on jumpers.

"People figure it must be some extended national holiday. Their Mailman hasn't shown up all week," a reporter wrote.

Malone's play was hardly unprecedented for a superstar. In the second game of the 1992 Finals against the Bulls, Portland's Clyde Drexler went into meltdown mode. One moment he threw up an air ball, the next Jordan glided past him for an easy basket.

A few minutes later, after a Chicago basket, Buck Williams grabbed the ball and stepped out of bounds for the inbounds play. He tossed it to Drexler, who inexplicably stepped out of bounds just as the ball reached him, producing a humiliating unforced turnover.

With four-and-a-half minutes remaining, Drexler fouled out and only then did the Blazers mount a game-winning drive.

Philadelphia columnist Bill Lyons wrote: "It has not so much to do with talent as it does with temperament. Jordan, by nature, will take a game and mold it in his hands and he will lash out at his teammates, goad them, and shame them. Drexler, by nature, is more passive. He will make the plays he can and assume the others will fall in dutifully behind."

Karl Malone's image took another beating as the series returned to the United Center for Game Three. Chicago was primed for a beating.

The tony Four Seasons Hotel slapped a Michael Jordan jersey on a statue in its entranceway. A downtown office building asked tenants to leave certain lights on at night and to turn others off - the result spelled out "Go Bulls" high above the city.

The *Chicago Tribune* ran a front-page story in the sports section about a ballboy who discovered the Bulls locker room was out of chewing gum a mere half hour before game-time. Because Jordan insists on chewing gum during games, the prescient ballboy saved the day.

Not that the Bulls needed saving.

After Game Three, Jerry Sloan was inspecting the box score. "This is actually the score? This is the final?"

It read Chicago 96, Utah 54. The Jazz had scored the fewest points in a NBA game since the inception of the shot clock in 1955.

"It's an embarrassment to all of us," Sloan said. "I take responsibility."

It wasn't the fault of the Mailman, who finished with 22 points on 8-of-11 shooting, but that hardly mattered to anyone in the Jazz lockerroom.

"We didn't come ready to play," Malone said. "If this doesn't wake us up, nothing will. You can't (blame the 10-day layoff). We got what we deserved, a whupping, a good old-fashioned one. We got no execution. We've got to respond as a team."

The Jazz had three days to think things over. So did the media, which questioned the Jazz' heart and will.

Rodman's low regard for the Jazz became obvious when he skipped practice on Monday to hang out with pro wrestler Hulk Hogan. When he showed up at Tuesday's practice, he proclaimed Malone couldn't beat him on the dribble. "He's just an average player to me," Rodman said.

In Game Four, Malone totalled 21 points and 14 rebounds, but when he went one-on-one with Rodman, he came up bust. In fact, the Mailman didn't make his first shot against The Worm until 4:46 remained in the third quarter. His only basket in the final quarter came with 9.1 seconds left.

And Rodman actually outscored him 5-2.

The key play: With 44 seconds left, Malone and Rodman positioned themselves for a rebound. But the Mailman couldn't grab for the ball because Rodman had tied him up under the basket and facing away from it. When Rodman reached for the rebound, Malone hauled him to the ground with his left arm and was whistled for a foul.

Rodman made two free throws to extend the Bulls' lead to 81-77.

"The much-maligned Dennis Rodman has done it again," Bulls coach Phil Jackson said after an 86-82 win. "He dug himself out of the hole he put himself in and redeemed himself. More than anything else, his defense on Karl was great."

Malone was reeling.

"I'm not going to get caught up in how many shots I've taken in the fourth quarter or how many I don't take," he said. "I've taken on my share in my career and I've taken plenty in the playoffs. This is just one of those things.

"I had opportunities to score on Dennis as well as Luc Longley and I just haven't. There's no excuse. In a situation like this, you guys have all the answers," he told reporters. "Everyone's an expert now. So I don't know if I answered that."

Not surprisingly, Chicago started preparing for the ultimate block party, just as it had done before Game Five against Phoenix in 1993.

Charles Barkley reined-in that parade by writing "Save the City" on the locker room blackboard shortly before the opening tip.

"The Jazz players were sitting in their hotel watching all the stories about Grant Park and the police telling people not to riot," Bulls guard Steve Kerr said. "The whole city seemed poised for a celebration and I'm sure it ticked them off."

Malone had to get away, so he and a friend, an Illinois state trooper, hopped on their motorcycles and headed for the hinterlands.

"You (media) guys laugh," he said. "I don't care what you guys do on your days off. It was a fun day for me and I enjoyed it."

Malone certainly enjoyed Game Five, picking up 39 points, nine rebounds and five assists during a stirring 83-81 win. Even more, he hit three clutch jumpers, including one from the left corner with 53 seconds left.

"You try not to listen to everything said about you because you know it's not so good, so you try not to read the paper," he said. "I was able to get away yesterday and get totally away from basketball and we, as a team, knew this was do-or-die."

Added Jordan: "Karl Malone carried them. And for all the criticism he's received in the playoffs, I think he put a lot of things to rest."

But it was the Mailman's last delivery.

In Game Six, the Jazz owned an 86-83 lead with 41 seconds left, thanks to a Stockton three-pointer. Jordan, however, raced upcourt to make it a one-point game. On the next possession, Malone had the ball on the low post, preparing to make a move. But Jordan stripped him of the ball, hurried up court, used a jab step to free himself from Bryon Russell and then fired another game-winning shot.

Malone had played in 137 career playoff games without winning an NBA title. Only one man can top that: John Stockton (147).

"It's the same thing, over and over, every year," Malone said after the 87-86 defeat. "I'm tired of it. I don't want to sign a basketball. I don't even want to see a basketball this summer."

But Malone didn't exactly go quietly into the summer.

In fact, he blasted two radio broadcasters, threatening to get them fired for criticizing him during the NBA Finals.

David Locke and former Jazz Coach Tom Nissalke were highly critical of Malone for missing shots and passing them up in the first four games of the Finals. Worst of all, Malone said, Locke compared him to Greg Norman, who blew a six-stroke lead in the final round of the 1996 Masters.

"I'll say this and I mean this: Either they shake that situation up at KFNZ with the two experts they got on that, or they've got to do something else with me. So it's me or them."

"What makes me most upset about the whole situation is KFNZ is owned by the Jazz," Malone added. "You don't hear guys in Chicago talking about their players like that, win or lose. You don't hear the Lakers talk about their players like that, win or lose.

"But, we have a couple experts at KFNZ - which is owned by the Jazz, and the Jazz sit back and say, 'Well, these guys are great at what they do.' What the hell? If they were so great, they'd have other jobs. That shade tree coach, ex-coach, whatever the hell he is. If he's such an expert, he'd have a job. And then a wannabe Jim Rome, the other guys. Please. And they're owned by the Jazz. They work for the Jazz. I don't understand that. So we'll fix it, though. We're gonna fix it."

The pugnacious Malone then turned his attention to pro wrestling and the hyping of a pay-per-view tag team match against Rodman on July 12 in San Diego. His partner was Diamond Dallas Page; Rodman's was Hulk Hogan.

On June 17 Malone and Rodman appeared on *The Tonight Show with Jay Leno* to hype the "Bash on the Beach."

"I called Karl a lot more than a wimp on the court,"

Rodman told Leno. "I don't know how he's going to beat me on the (mat.)"

Just as Rodman was saying that, Malone and Page strutted onto the stage, triggering raucous cheering from the audience. Malone, who was wearing a sleeveless World Championship Wrestling shirt, stuck a playful headlock on Leno.

Malone's wrestling debut upset many NBA traditionalists, including NBC play-by-play man Bob Costas, who wondered aloud why the Mailman would "lower himself" to this.

Many Jazz fans agreed, which angered Malone.

"I've always wanted to wrestle, ever since I was a little kid," he said.

"If Karl Malone is in LA or New York, it'd be no big deal," he said. "But everything I do or say, I'm headlines in Utah."

Jazz management sent him a letter, warning a wrestling injury would void his contract, which got under his collar as well.

But that didn't stop him from stepping into the ring, accompanied by head-banging rock music and raucous cheers. Rodman and Hogan "won," but only after "The Disciple," a friend of Hogan's, sneaked into the ring to distract Malone's team, allowing Hogan to pin Page.

That made the Mailman very angry. He grabbed Rodman's and Hogan's heads, and smashed them together. Then he snorted, stomped, etc.

Malone's wrestling debut didn't disgust everyone in Salt Lake City.

An editorial in the *Salt Lake Tribune* opined: "From the reaction of some sports fans to Jazz star Karl Malone's foray into professional wrestling, one would think that NBA, NFL and NHL athletes have signed some sort of Hippocratic oath instead of multi-million dollar contracts to play for professional sports franchises. Face it fans, professional (athletes) get paid gazillions of dollars every year to push, poke, tackle and high-stick each other ...(Malone) loved wrestling as a child; he loves it as an adult. He's not breaking any laws by wrestling. Lighten up."

The Summer of Controversy didn't end there.

Malone surprised Jazz officials when he hired Dwight Manley, Rodman's agent, as his agent. They used words such as "dangerous" and "explosive" privately to describe upcoming negotiations.

Malone is scheduled to earn $6 million in the 1998-99 season, which is well below market value for a player of his stature. When he becomes a free agent on July 1, 1999, he could command three to four times as much.

"A lot of things have happened this summer and started me thinking, 'What does Karl Malone want to do with his life?' A lot of things this summer have been said and done that could have an effect on my staying in Utah. I'm going to weigh all of those," he told ESPN.

When ESPN's Chris Meyers suggested that Malone sounded like a player on his way out, he said, "I hope it never comes to that. But I'm preparing for the worst. I'm not saying (leaving Utah) is the worst thing that happened. But it would be a sad day."

Malone's tumultuous off-season continued when he assumed a prominent role in the Players Association controversial labor negotiations with the NBA. And in November, as the NBA lockout continued, Malone dropped another bomb when he announced he wanted out of Salt Lake City immediately. This time there was no confusion about his message: He announced his intentions on his own Los Angeles-based radio show.

Jazz fans remained hopeful the Mailman would bring home an NBA title before he moved on to the next phase of his life.

But only one thing seemed certain: The Karl Malone Story is far from being over. In fact, in the Mailman's mind, it's only beginning.